PARENTING AUTISTIC CHILDREN: NAVIGATING THE SPECTRUM

HELP THEM THROUGH MELTDOWNS, FOSTER SOCIAL SKILLS, MANAGE SPECIAL EDUCATION PLANS, AND ADVOCATE FOR THE SERVICES THEY DESERVE

MICHAEL STEVENS

CONTENTS

INTRODUCTION

"It would be easier to teach the class if your daughter wasn't in it."

These are words every parent of a child with special needs hopes they don't hear at an Individual Education Plan meeting, even if they suspect that that's what the teachers are thinking. I actually heard those words at what would be my daughter Lizzie's last IEP meeting in a public school. She was in eighth grade and failing everything by September.

After the meeting, I was so mad I couldn't even cry. I immediately began researching other options, because public schooling couldn't help her anymore. It was at that moment that I knew I needed to do more. Not just for her, but for others in the same situation.

I was able to find her a school where she could begin to thrive. This school had educators who specialized in children with special needs, small class sizes, and they genuinely cared about her. I know not every parent will be able to find this kind of school for their child due to location, cost, or a host of other factors, but I hope that in these pages, you find the strength to advocate for your child in education and mental health, to give your autistic child every opportunity to find their niche and watch them shine.

When people think about someone like Temple Grandin, their minds usually go to her outstanding career as a scientist and designer in spite of her autism. It is less common that they think of autism as one of the keys to her career, or that her successful career was possible because her mother, disregarding medical advice, decided to nurture her strengths instead of giving up on her because of her specific needs.

In a time when autism was a newly identified condition and institutionalization was the recommended treatment, Grandin's mother took upon herself the task of providing her daughter with the therapy, environment, and support that she needed. And while Temple did not have an easy journey, her mother's support was crucial in the development of her abilities and skills. Her willingness to encourage her daughter's interests and creativity paved the way for Temple to pursue working in the cattle industry and to become a world-renowned expert in the humane handling of animals.

As a spokesperson for people on the autism spectrum, Grandin has always emphasized the need for parents and caretakers to provide their autistic children with skills of all kinds. "Teach them language," she said in a 2023 interview, "Teach them how to take turns at games, and teach them skills, like putting on clothing. The worst thing you can do with a child who's not talking at age two or three is do nothing and let them zone out on electronics. Now, when the kids get a little older, we need to be looking more at what they can do. A lot of those who remain non-verbal have more skills than you think they might have. Build on the thing the kid is good at" (Keltner, 2023).

But, for her, teaching skills to children is only the beginning. Exposure is an elemental part of developing the child's interests: "Kids have to be exposed to things to find out what they might be good at. I feel so strongly that schools made a big mistake when they took out all the hands-on classes because I was super good at art. Well, that's not gonna show up if art is never encouraged. For another kid, it might be music. And work on what they're good at. I'm very much into a career. Students get interested in what they are exposed to. I got interested in the cattle industry because I was exposed to it as a teenager" (Keltner, 2023).

Temple Grandin's life story is a story of resilience but is also a teaching of the key role parents of autistic children play in equipping them for life and the future.

This, of course, is not an easy task. Autism, though nowadays highly researched and documented, is still permeated by a negative social stigma as a result of misinformation and ignorance. A general lack of awareness can result in misguided and erroneous advice and interference that not only isolate autistic individuals and those who care for them but also add an extra burden to parents who struggle every day with the emotional toll of being the main advocates for their children's well-being.

As with any condition that functions on a spectrum, an autism diagnosis can be a complicated and lengthy process, riddled with fear and uncertainty, and unfortunate experiences can create in the parents a sense of mistrust of healthcare professionals. Added to the lack of social empathy, the financial strain of necessary therapies, and the attention to their child's special needs, parenting an autistic child can take a toll on inner family relationships.

While autism can be a complex condition, many of these issues stem from ignorance, misinformation, and social stigma. Differences in opinions and variations in autism knowledge among healthcare professionals and teachers can make the navigation of the medical and educational world a struggle. As someone who has been in that exact position and has encountered the same struggles, I want to provide parents with a set of tools, practical solutions, and strategies that can assist them in this journey.

This book is meant to be a guide, to assist you in your daily life and the challenges that come with it, be it in your home, at school, at the doctor's office, and in every other setting where you need a helping hand. It will cover from first signs and early diagnosis to understanding your child's personal and unique needs and how to make your home a comfortable and safe space. It will discuss emotions, behaviors, social skills, autonomy, and independence in everyday life and the transition from childhood to adulthood. It will tackle navigating the healthcare and education systems, being the main advocate for your child, and helping them set up for the future and for any circumstances that might arise. Lastly, but no less important, it will focus on the parents and the importance of a healthy mindset, self-care, and support systems.

Autism as a condition is not an obstacle to a successful and happy life, and there are multiple examples of this. Just to quote one: Elon Musk has attributed part of his success to having autism, even if he did not have the happiest of childhoods. Despite the bullying he received and his struggle to understand social cues that were intuitive for his peers, he found an interest in science and technology. For him, autism played a key role in intensifying that interest, which in turn led him to specialize in it and make a career out of it. Like Temple Grandin's story, Elon Musk is an example of the possibilities that arise for people on the autism spectrum when they work with their brain and not against it.

As a specialist with a focus on autism but, most importantly, as a father of a daughter with autism, I have been where you are, and I have come across the same obstacles with diagnosis, school systems, healthcare providers, and social interactions. It is from this insight that I want to provide you with the tools that you might need to succeed in this journey of parenting.

CHAPTER 1

EARLY SIGNS AND DIAGNOSIS

Autism has been studied as a condition since the first decades of the 20th century, but only in 1943 was the term systematically used to diagnose children who showed socially withdrawn and isolated behaviors. The severity of the reported symptoms meant that children with milder signs were less likely to be diagnosed, but the progressive broadening of the criteria since then has contributed to expanding the definition and the diagnosis of autism spectrum disorder (ASD), which has resulted in earlier diagnoses and access to proper care.

RECOGNIZING SIGNS OF AUTISM

The core symptoms of autism can be divided into two main sections: social communication challenges and restricted and repetitive behaviors. These symptoms can manifest in different ways according to age, severity of the condition, and personal circumstances, but there are some reoccurring signs that you can look for.

ASD in Young Children

Autism in infants and toddlers can manifest as:

- avoiding eye contact
- not responding to their name
- not smiling when smiled at and not showing facial expressions of sadness, anger, happiness, or surprise
- exhibiting repetitive behaviors (e.g., flapping their hands, spinning in circles, flicking their fingers, running back and forth, or rocking their body)
- talking less than other children their age or not talking at all; repeating certain words and phrases constantly
- using few or no gestures appropriate for their age (e.g., waving their hands, pointing)
- getting upset by minor changes or certain tastes, smells, and sounds
- not engaging in pretend play or simple interactive games

ASD in Older Children

Symptoms in older children may include:

- difficulty in recognizing emotions in themselves and others
- feeling overwhelmed in social situations
- adhering to a strict daily routine
- getting upset at changes in their routine or directions

- unusual speech patterns (e.g., echolalia), or not talking at all
- having an obsessive interest in specific topics
- having a literal understanding; having difficulty understanding sarcasm, jokes, sayings, or double meanings
- having difficulty understanding social cues, conventions, or physical language
- exhibiting repetitive motions with objects (e.g., clicking switches, spinning wheels) or ritualistic behaviors (touching things in a set order, lining up objects)
- having difficulty connecting with their peers and forming friendships; preferring to be on their own

ASD in Girls and Boys

Autism has been historically underdiagnosed in girls and women due to stereotypes and biased assumptions. Girls with ASD are also more likely to mask their autistic traits, which in turn leads them to be misdiagnosed or their symptoms to be confused with those of co-occurring conditions.

Although girls and women on the autistic spectrum usually perform better in social situations, it is important that they receive a proper and accurate diagnosis so that they can access the support and therapy that they need. The criteria and tools used to reach a diagnosis tend to account for characteristics that are more common in men and boys, so doctors and other healthcare professionals need to be informed and educated about the different presentations of autism in women, increasing the chances of an accurate diagnosis.

Some key differences in presentation to be aware of:

- Autistic girls might mask their behaviors by copying their peers.
- When presented with difficult situations, autistic girls and women are more likely to withdraw instead of externalizing their feelings.
- Interests and repetitive behaviors in autistic girls tend to be similar to those of non-autistic girls (e.g., twirling their hair, reading, writing), but they display a higher focus and intensity.
- Autistic girls and women are more likely to have fewer social difficulties than their male counterparts and are more likely to be part of social groups.

DEVELOPMENT DELAYS

Though ASD symptoms vary from child to child, certain developmental delays can be a sign of autism and appear as early as the first year. It is important to note some children might reach their developmental milestones through infancy but slowly, as they get older, stop their development or even regress.

In addition to repetitive behaviors, sensory issues, and fixations, it is important to detect a significant delay in reaching social milestones:

- **Nine months of age:** Not responding to their name. Not displaying facial signs of emotion.

- **Twelve months of age:** Not engaging in interactive play. Using few or no physical gestures (pointing, waving, tugging).
- **Fifteen months of age:** Not sharing interests with others (e.g., showing someone a thing that they like).
- **Eighteen months of age:** Not looking at something being pointed at.
- **Twenty-four months of age:** Being unable to identify other people's emotions (sadness, hurt, anger).
- **Thirty months of age:** Not engaging in pretend play.
- **Three years or older:** Not being able to understand other people's feelings or having difficulty expressing their own. Not being able to say their name when asked, ask basic questions, or maintain a simple conversation (at least two exchanges).
- **Five years:** Having difficulty with games and activities that involve taking turns.

It is important to note that, even if children on the autistic spectrum usually experience developmental delays, not all delays are a sign of autism, as some children might miss a milestone but catch up to their peers later. A serious developmental delay can be a condition of its own, with no relation whatsoever to ASD. Nevertheless, children with any kind of developmental delay will benefit from early detection and intervention.

My daughter Lizzie didn't start walking until she was nearly 18 months old. We just thought she preferred to be carried.

However, looking back on it, this was an early sign of development delays related to autism. She was our first-born and the first-born grandchild on my wife's side of the family. So, we carried her a lot, and so did other people in our family. However, when she was on the ground, she never tried walking. We would show her and do things you're supposed to do when teaching a baby to walk.

She didn't start showing interest in trying to walk until between 18 and 24 months old. Eventually, she got the hang of it, but well past when children generally learn to walk. When she was learning to talk, it was a similar story. She didn't try to say words, and she didn't babble like many toddlers. She would stare at the face of the person talking but wouldn't try to respond or mimic words until she was nearly two years old. Again, we assumed she was just concentrating very hard and didn't want to try until she felt she could say the words. We didn't realize this was also a developmental delay and was a feature of autism.

Due to some of these delays with her speech, she wasn't communicating well enough by the time she turned five and had to be held back from starting Kindergarten until she turned six.

Mikey's Story:

Mikey was diagnosed with severe ASD at age four. By age eight, third-grader Mikey had been receiving occupational therapy at school for two years but still had difficulty with social interactions with peers and siblings. His parents noted that he'd been having problems with his morning routine, which in turn affects his mood all day, causing troubles in school.

Mikey's parents requested a home evaluation and recommendations from an occupational therapist to help with these issues. The therapist conducted three home visits where she observed Mikey's routine during the morning and the night of a school day. She noted that Mikey didn't react well when awakened by loud noises, which resulted in having issues with his morning routine, his schoolwork, and his relationships with his classmates. He had trouble sleeping at night and appeared fatigued during the day but was unable to nap. Mikey was also unable to play or share toys with his sister and exhibited repetitive behaviors such as spinning a particular toy or switching the lights on and off repeatedly.

The therapist concluded that Mikey's levels of cooperation, imitation, interest, ability to adopt a role, and motor skills were below those of a five-year-old and that he had delays related to registration, attention, and sensory processing. She suggested that Mikey could benefit from intensive occupational therapy outside of school to manage his symptoms and that his home would be the least restrictive environment for this therapy. Her goal was to help Mikey go through his morning routine without meltdowns and to get him to participate in interactive play.

Mikey started therapy at home five days a week, and his therapist focused on helping him assess his emotions and his responses to trigger situations. After assessing his level of emotion, they focused on strategies to avoid meltdowns and drastic responses to allow Mikey to incorporate adaptive skills in his routine, such as calmly going to a quiet place when overwhelmed or asking his sister to stop crying instead of running away from her. The therapist also made Mikey practice his motor skills, created a picture schedule of his morning routine, and gave his parents a weighted blanket as a device to help Mikey regulate his emotions.

The therapist had conversations with Mikey's parents to explain his sensory issues and how specific situations might cause meltdowns and tantrums, and suggested changes in the home's environment (such as a softer-sounding alarm or sound-absorbing panels in Mikey's room) and in the family's environment (such as the family learning to identify which objects and sounds were potential triggers for Mikey). Additionally, she suggested hippotherapy and a social skills training program.

RED FLAGS FOR AUTISM SPECTRUM DISORDER (ASD)

Children develop at their own pace, but delays in certain milestones might be red flags for autism. These delays are not enough for a diagnosis in themselves, but they are taken into consideration for further assessments:

- no words by 18 months or no combination of words by 24 months
- no pointing or gestures
- not responding to their name
- inconsistent eye contact
- inability to divide their attention back and forth between persons and objects

- losing language skills that they had previously mastered
- unusual repetitive behaviors with their hands or other body parts
- interest and attachment to random objects

If you notice any of these behaviors in your child, the best course of action is to consult your pediatrician. Even if there's not enough evidence for an autism diagnosis, early intervention will help to improve a skill that is lacking.

HOW DO DOCTORS DIAGNOSE ASD?

Early diagnosis can make a huge difference when it comes to autism spectrum disorder, both for the children and their families, but it's not an easy diagnosis to make, as there is no test for it. Due to the wide array of possible symptoms, doctors have to rely on the behavior they can observe and the input and concerns from parents and caregivers. As a condition on a spectrum, autism can present with varying degrees of severity and can be diagnosed as early as two years old, though some signs might present earlier.

Autism diagnosis has two stages:

1. **Well-child visits:** The diagnosis process will always start with your pediatrician, so if you have concerns, this is the moment to voice them. They will assess your child at their 18 and 24-month-old checkups to make sure they are on track with their development. They will ask you about milestones (such as if your baby smiles, babbles, mimics

expressions) and about their behavior (if they interact with others, if they have repetitive or unusual behaviors, if they answer to their name). They will also want to know about any possible sensitivities to light, sounds, and temperature and if they have issues sleeping or eating. It is important to inform your doctor of any family history of ASD or other disorders (such as ADHD, learning disorders, or intellectual disabilities).

2. **Further testing:** If needed, your pediatrician might refer you to other specialists for additional tests. This could mean visiting a child psychologist, a speech therapist, an occupational therapist, a developmental pediatrician, or a neurologist to assess your child's cognitive level, language, or life skills.

Remember that to obtain an official diagnosis, according to the *Diagnostic and Statistical Manual of Mental Disorders* (*DSM-5*), your child must have problems in two main categories: communication and social interaction, and restrictive and repetitive patterns of behavior. If their symptoms are insufficient for a proper diagnosis, your pediatrician will monitor their evolution and recommend any additional therapy and testing to encourage development and rule out other conditions.

GETTING A SECOND OPINION

ASD can vary its presentation and severity from person to person. Added to this, the lack of lab tests for it can make its diagnosis very challenging. This might lead to a missed, incorrect, or late diagnosis.

Jane's Story

Jane has been in therapy since she was 16 years old due to depression and anxiety connected with socializing issues and bullying. At 18 years old, she received an ASD diagnosis that she felt was rushed and not properly tested. When voicing her concerns to her doctor, she was told that autism was a fitting diagnosis for her socializing issues. The diagnosis not only left Jane unsatisfied but also led her to doubt herself and her perception of the world around her.

At 21 years old, Jane decided to advocate for herself and asked for a second opinion. She visited an adult ADHD specialist who, through extensive testing and in a respectful manner, diagnosed her with severe ADHD and confirmed that her prior diagnosis was indeed rushed and incorrect. With the help of therapy and medication, Jane was able to socialize, go to university, get a good job, and lead a peaceful life.

ASD can co-occur with other conditions, many of which have overlapping symptoms. This not only makes diagnosing more difficult but also increases the chances of an incorrect diagnosis. Jane's story is an example of the importance of trusting your feelings, even if that means going against the opinion of a professional.

As a parent or caregiver, remember that you know your child best, and advocating for them is your responsibility. If you believe your child has been misdiagnosed or you feel that your healthcare professional has dismissed your concerns, consider getting a second opinion, as a late or incorrect diagnosis will delay your child's access to proper therapy and support.

THE BENEFITS OF EARLY DIAGNOSIS AND INTERVENTIONS

The "Plastic" Brain

Professionals emphasize the importance of early intervention due to neuroplasticity (that is, the brain's ability to form new connections). Although our brains never lose this ability, they have a better capacity for it during infancy and childhood when our brains are still developing. Studies have shown that early intervention in the form of speech, occupational and behavioral therapy, and special education can greatly improve the development of autistic children in comparison with their peers who received a later diagnosis.

Autism Prevention

Is it possible to prevent autism? Not yet. But what we can do is to ensure the earliest possible diagnosis and intervention to allow the brain's neuroplasticity to develop the skills it is lacking. With this goal in mind, autism specialists have developed a series of criteria that would allow them to evaluate children between 6 and 12 months old, and they have focused their efforts on children whose siblings have ASD.

Research has shown that some of these children (who were later on also diagnosed) could present signs of autism as young as six months old: they were passive, had low muscle tone, were unable to sit independently, and had issues developing motor skills, while others didn't show any symptoms at that age. At the one-year-old mark, however, all showed apparent behavioral signs and socializing and communication issues. While ASD is typically diagnosed around the two-year-old mark, these criteria allowed investigators to make a correct diagnosis around the 14-month-old mark.

The researchers then developed an intervention program suited for children that age that focused on helping the parents cope with their child's unique needs, taught them how to play and interact with the children to promote skill development, and used the nursery school setting to develop socialization and communication skills.

Early Intervention: What's It All About?

All experts agree that the earlier the intervention begins, the better. They don't agree, however, on what form the intervention should take. There are two major approaches:

- **Behavioral approaches:** This kind of intervention uses Applied Behavior Analysis (ABA), which involves a more structured teaching where children are rewarded for the goals achieved and the skills learned.
- **Developmental approaches:** These interventions include focusing on certain skills or behaviors, but emphasize the integration of the child into the

environment and the development of social relationships.

Both approaches can be complemented with therapy and medications according to the specific needs of each child.

Hunter's Story

Though Hunter seemed a typical infant, his parents suspected that his meltdowns and tantrums were beyond what was typical for a child his age. He was particularly sensitive to certain textures and had irregular sleeping patterns.

While seeking an ASD diagnosis, his mother decided to start him with different therapies. Hunter received a diagnosis at age three, and by age six, he was integrated with his peers, had no issues making friends, and was able to identify and express most of his feelings. His meltdowns have not disappeared but have greatly improved, showing that while early intervention might not completely remove all ASD symptoms, it is crucial in improving them and helping children and parents access a better quality of life.

As we have seen, the varying degrees of severity and the different presentations of the symptoms can make diagnosing autism a complex issue, but paying attention to your child's development and advocating for their needs is key in ensuring they get the earliest possible access to any help and support they might need.

CHAPTER 2
UNDERSTANDING YOUR CHILD'S UNIQUE NEEDS

SEEING THE WORLD DIFFERENTLY

People with autism spectrum disorder not only experience developmental delays, socializing issues, or repetitive behaviors, but the way they see and process the world around them is fundamentally different from someone who is not on the spectrum. Their sensory systems are much more sensitive than normal, which can lead to sensory overload as they try to process the influx of information from their environment. This can cause tantrums and anxiety and make them socially withdrawn.

Research has shown that people with ASD have a higher sensitivity to visual motion in their peripheral field of vision. This not only has an influence on how they perceive their surroundings and how they situate themselves in time and space, but also affects their motor skills and their coordination.

While people not on the spectrum rely on their vision to adjust their posture and movement and can learn to ignore peripheral movement, people with autism have problems making this distinction and tend to confuse peripheral movement with self-movement.

Mark's Story

Mark was diagnosed with autism when he was five years old. At age 17, he goes to high school, has a tight-knit group of friends, and enjoys playing video games. Although occupational therapy has helped him immensely in developing life skills and socializing, he still struggles in these areas.

When asked by his friends how it feels to be on the spectrum, Mark answers that he feels like everyone else has a rule book for life from which they have learned how to socialize, read social cues, and interpret feelings, while he hasn't been given that book. He has to go through life guessing while, at the same time, the world is at its loudest volume.

With the help of his family and the tools provided by therapy, Mark has an easier time navigating social situations. Most of the time, he knows when to push himself and when to go back to a safe, calm place if he's feeling overwhelmed, but the world around him still feels loud and bright.

THE AUTISM SPECTRUM

As a condition on a spectrum, autism is inherently complex. While researchers and healthcare professionals have made progress in defining and determining autism levels, there are still generalizations and simplifications that can lead to misunderstandings and be detrimental to people with ASD.

The terms "low-functioning autism" and "high-functioning autism" have been extensively used to describe persons on the spectrum according to the level of support they need in their daily lives, but they are inaccurate and can cause confusion.

Labeling individuals as low or high-functioning creates the idea that the autistic spectrum is composed of two positions: one that performs well alone and one that doesn't. The term "spectrum" refers to the span of symptoms that can present in the condition and does not determine the ability to function, the intelligence level, the sensitivity, or the talents of any autistic person. Someone considered high-functioning might have an easier time in social settings but struggle with their job or their studies, while someone deemed as low-functioning might be non-verbal but extremely talented and intelligent.

To avoid these misleading labels, the *Diagnostic and Statistical Manual of Mental Disorders (DSM-5)* diagnoses the severity of the condition using levels (1, 2, or 3) that describe the amount of support each person requires without making assumptions about their personal characteristics.

Sarah's Story

Sarah received her ASD diagnosis during her teenage years. Her teachers describe her as someone high-functioning, smart, and sociable. While Sarah might function well in the school setting, she struggles to interact with people she doesn't know and be in other public spaces. She dislikes the use of the term "high-functioning" as she feels it invalidates her struggles as an autistic person and leads other people to expect certain behaviors from her.

NEURODIVERSITY AND AUTISM

Neurodiversity addresses the idea that humans are not neurologically equal due to variations in the human genome. While neurodiversity aims to be inclusive as a movement, it can present some issues.

The neurodiversity movement began in 1998 when activist Judy Singer coined the term and argued that neurological conditions were a normal variation of the human genome. She saw these differences as beneficial to the diversity of the world and as a presentation of unusual skills and aptitudes.

When talking specifically about autism, neurodiversity doesn't see it as a disorder but as a neurological difference that entails a unique way of seeing and experiencing the world. From this follows that people on the autistic spectrum shouldn't be treated any differently and that society should accommodate them and promote a greater understanding of their differences.

Neurodiversity has greatly benefited autistic people by promoting equality while avoiding segregating them from society; it has encouraged an understanding of autism and other neurological conditions that embraces the differences and rejects the "suffering" approach usually associated with disabilities. The neurodiversity movement puts a special emphasis on the language around autism in an effort to reduce the negative traits associated with the condition.

However, the movement has received criticism due to the issues not being addressed. Many people believe that this view promotes the idea of the "autistic genius" and erases those on the spectrum who require extensive support or who don't live up to the exceptional qualities expected from them.

THE TRUTH ABOUT SAVANTS

Savant syndrome is a rare condition in which individuals with neurological conditions display amazing talents and abilities. These skills coexist with conditions such as autism, genetic disorders, brain malformations, or intellectual disabilities, among others. While in the case of other disabilities savant skills represent less than 1% of the individuals, approximately 1 in 10 autistic persons have some savant skills (The Treffert Center, 2021).

Savant skills include a spectrum of abilities, such as incredible memorization, musical, artistic, or mathematical expertise, linguistic skills, or outstanding knowledge in a particular field, to name a few. In some cases, these abilities can be channeled and expanded, but in others, these are splinter skills, meaning that they are extremely specific and not always useful in day-to-day life.

While the presence of savant skills in autistic people is higher than in other neurological conditions, this does not mean that all autistic savants will display these skills at an extraordinary level. "Talented" and "Prodigious" savants, though being the most portrayed in books and films, are a minority, and these representations have contributed to

misconceptions and stereotypes about autism and its characteristics.

THE AUTISTIC BRAIN

Even though ASD is diagnosed based on behaviors
(restricted, repetitive behaviors, and social and communication challenges), these traits are believed to be a result of
brain development. Researchers were unable to uncover a
specific pattern of changes when it comes to autism, as there
seems to be a variety across individuals, but they have
noticed the emergence of some trends that might, later on,
give us insights into the functioning of autism and help with
the development of new treatments.

Studies have shown that there are some structural differences between autistic and non-autistic people regarding
their brain structure. Autistic children and adolescents
usually present a bigger hippocampus (the area that forms
and stores memories), and all autistic individuals seem to
have smaller amygdala's and decreased amounts of brain
tissue in parts of the cerebellum. Their cortex (which is the
brain's outer layer) also seems to be thinner.

In addition to all these structural differences, researchers
have also registered differences in development during
childhood and even in early adulthood and have suggested
that the connection between the different regions of the
brain presents alterations in people with ASD. It is less clear
if these characteristics have some connection with sex due to
autism being underdiagnosed in girls.

Though these studies have not yet reached definitive conclusions, their development might be helpful in reaching earlier diagnoses and identifying autism subtypes.

WHEN YOU FEEL YOU'VE FAILED AS A PARENT

Parenting is a job like no other. As a parent, you are the main person responsible for the safety, happiness, and education of your child and the decision-maker on all issues regarding them until they reach an age where they can assume that responsibility. It is a difficult role and one that, more often than not, can come accompanied by worries and feelings of guilt. And while guilt can sometimes be powerful in motivating us to do the right thing and avoid past mistakes, it can also be incapacitating when taken to an extreme.

This is true for all parents, but especially for parents whose children have special needs. On top of the usual worries of any parent, they have the added uncertainty of diagnoses, the lack of knowledge about the conditions, and the extra support their kids need. They have to face feelings of fear and helplessness and move through the grief that comes with accepting their child's conditions and handicaps.

As a parent of a child on the spectrum, you might feel crushed under the weight of decisions that have high stakes: early interventions, therapies, abilities to nurture, and planning for the future. Every decision might make you question if you are doing the right thing as your child's advocate. You might feel guilty due to self-blame, past mistakes, or negative thoughts, and you might feel that you are not doing enough to avoid your child's suffering. If your children are older, your relationship with them suffers due to conflicting ideas on what's best to do.

It is necessary to recognize the presence and the power of guilt in order to move forward through it. As a parent, you must remember that you have your own feelings and personal struggles and that processing those feelings will allow you to reduce the weight that they might have over your decision-making.

If you are trying to do what's best for your child, you are not failing as a parent. You are learning as you go, and you are doing your best to support your child so they can develop and progress to the best of their abilities. Guilt and frustration are a natural part of this process, and as long as you are able to recognize these feelings and work through them, you will be the most important ally and supporter of your child.

SUPPORT GROUPS

Having a support network is not only crucial but also profoundly impactful for both individuals on the autism spectrum and their families. While friends and relatives undoubtedly provide invaluable support, there's a unique resonance in connecting with others who share similar experiences and challenges.

Local support groups serve as vital conduits for fostering such connections. They offer a safe, understanding, and non-judgmental environment where individuals with autism can interact freely, forge friendships, and develop crucial social skills. These groups not only benefit the individuals themselves but also serve as invaluable resources for parents and caregivers. Through sharing experiences and strategies, parents can find solace, advice, and solidarity with others navigating similar journeys.

In addition to the emotional support they provide, many local support groups offer practical resources. This can range from access to occupational and speech therapy services to connections with healthcare professionals and special educators.

To facilitate access to these networks, organizations such as *The Autism Society of North Carolina* (www.autismsociety-nc.org) and *The Autism Project* (www.theautismproject.org) offer interactive online platforms where individuals and families can find local support groups tailored to their needs and preferences. Moreover, initiatives like *Making Autistic Friendships* (www.makingauthenticfriendships.com) and *Friend in Me* (www.friendinmegroup.org) focus specifically on cultivating connections between individuals on the autism spectrum and their neurotypical peers, fostering inclusivity and understanding within broader social circles. Through these avenues, individuals and families can not only find support but also actively participate in building more inclusive and supportive communities.

It is important to remember that autistic individuals have a unique way of viewing the world and interpreting the information from their environment. On the other hand, we also need to consider that autism is not a uniform condition and that its presentation and symptoms vary from person to person. Recognizing these differences is key to understanding that every person on the spectrum will have unique needs and requirements. As a parent, being aware of your child's unique needs will help you provide them with the best resources, support, and safe spaces.

CHAPTER 3

A SENSORY-FRIENDLY HOME

Human beings receive and process information from around them through their senses. But for people with sensory processing issues (like many of those on the spectrum), this can mean they are constantly overwhelmed by an environment that is too loud, too bright, too fast-moving, and more. It is important that they have controlled spaces at home where they can feel safe and rested.

CREATING SENSORY SAFE SPACES

Sensory triggers vary from person to person, but there are certain things that you can do to ensure that your child's space and other spaces at home are calm and intentionally understated.

- Use soft, diffused, or adjustable lights. Consider the amount of natural light in the space and whether you will need blinds or blackout curtains.
- Avoid bold and bright colors, and paint the rooms in neutral or pastel shades.

- Noisy floors can be toned down with rugs and mats, but make sure that they are anchored to avoid slipping.
- Prioritize low and close to the floor furniture, such as coffee tables, cushions, bean bags, and low chairs.
- If your child needs extra sensory stimulation, create a space with sensory toys that can be squeezed, pulled, rolled, or pushed and toys or plushies that are comfortable to hug.
- A transition chart or a list can be helpful if your child struggles to go from one activity to the other.
- Include your child's interests in the books, toys, and décor chosen, and make sure to include them in decisions about colors, themes, and furniture if they have a preference.
- Design the spaces with your child's safety in mind, no matter their age. Arrange the furniture to create pathways and make sure there are no easily breakable items or choking hazards.
- Calming sounds, music, and aromatherapy can be helpful tools, but make sure that they are not a trigger for your child.
- Try to avoid extra décor elements such as ornaments or wall hangings that could cause clutter.
- Sound-absorbing panels and materials, noise-canceling headphones, and earplugs are helpful if your child tends to get overwhelmed by noise.
- When choosing furniture and materials, prioritize comfortable and easy-to-clean options.

Johnny's Story

Johnny is an autistic toddler with a need for sensory stimulation. His parents want to equip his room according to his needs, but they don't know how. They decide to take to an online forum for autistic parents and ask for age-appropriate suggestions.

Based on the advice received, they decided to include a light projector, a swing, and a wall activity panel. They make sure to include comfortable pillows and a cozy rug, and they have a weighted blanket should Johnny need it.

As Johnny has a tendency to chew things, they make sure to avoid toys with smaller parts, or soft squishable items.

THE BENEFITS OF A SENSORY ROOM FOR AUTISTIC CHILDREN

Sensory rooms are a great tool for autistic children to explore and interact with their environment in a safe and controlled way that is consistent, risk-free, and that allows them to easily introduce new elements or remove unwanted ones.

These are some of the benefits of having a sensory room:

- They are an opportunity for interaction. Be it in your house, a school, or a daycare, sensory rooms encourage socialization skills and interactive play in a calm environment.
- Sensory rooms can help autistic children work their gross and fine motor skills, improve their movement

and coordination, and better their muscle tone. It can also be a calming place where they can relax.

- A calming environment is the best place for a child to practice their concentration. Some sensory toys are designed to help with focusing and engaging with activities.
- A good sensory room should stimulate all five senses. The controlled environment is a perfect space to help your children naturally increase their tolerance to stimuli at their own pace.
- Sensory rooms are a place of learning but also relaxation and play. By engaging the children's interests, sensory toys and games aid them in developing their skills and their senses. The relaxing environment will give them a place to decompress if they are overwhelmed, tired, or have a meltdown as they learn to self-regulate their behaviors and emotions.

WAYS TO CREATE A SENSORY ROOM ON A BUDGET

There are some great sensory toys and gadgets on the market, but we can't always afford to build a sensory room from scratch. But there are ways to do it with a limited budget and utilizing things that we already own.

- **Movement:** Instead of a swing, children can practice their balance using a rocking chair, a bouncing ball, or a mini trampoline.
- **Lighting:** String lights, battery-powered candles, lava lamps, and glow sticks are some of the low-

budget lighting options that you can use to create soft lighting.

- **Tactile and sensory items:** You don't need to purchase special items. Focus on toys and objects that you already own that have interesting textures, movements, or sounds.

- **Therapeutic scents:** If you want to try aromatherapy but are hesitant about buying an oil diffuser, you can introduce your child to calming scents by adding essential oils to a cotton ball.

- **Tactile wall:** Tactile walls can be easily created with household elements that are visually and tactilely interesting.

- **Crash pad:** Crash pads are used to stimulate proprioception (our body's ability to locate its own parts, how they move, and how much strength we need) by jumping and crashing on it. Instead of purchasing a pad, you can stuff a duvet cover with pillows and blankets.

- **Vibration sensory input:** A hand-held massager can be as helpful as a massage mat or expensive vibrating equipment.

- **Music:** Instead of a sound system, use your phone, a speaker, or a stereo that you already own.

- **Deep pressure:** Instead of building a snuggle space you can reduce costs by filling a tent or a kiddie pool with blankets and stuffed animals. You can also use a thick duvet or several blankets as a replacement for a weighted blanket.

Abe's Story

Abe is 12 years old and has autism. He is moderately verbal and interacts minimally with his peers, but he is slow to respond to instructions or calls from others. His parents are concerned about his behavior, as he has recently started touching his private areas and smearing feces in public. He hasn't had his hair cut in a long time and has also refused to let the dentist check his teeth. Neither his parents nor his teachers have been able to identify any triggers for these behaviors. They used to be able to hold him and calm him by applying pressure, but he has gained strength recently and refuses to sit still.

After getting a referral to an autism center, Abe was assessed by professionals who concluded that these behaviors stemmed from a mix of sensory issues:

- Abe's refusal to let someone cut his hair or check his teeth showed he was hypersensitive to touch, especially if it was light and unpredictable. His recent behaviors seemed to be both triggered by noise (they occurred in places like the classroom, shops, or the zoo) and used as a way to escape these places because he knew parents and teachers would remove him from there.
- Abe's low response to others showed he was underresponsive to verbal auditory stimuli, which was worsened by his limited understanding of verbal language. However, he was very responsive when parents and teachers used visual strategies.

- Abe's touching, his smearing of feces, and his enjoyment of playing with water showed that he was seeking tactile input that he could control (as opposed to tactile input from others). He felt under-stimulated in that sense during class, which added to his being overwhelmed by noise and triggered his behavior.

The healthcare professionals suggested the following strategies:

- Add tactile activities to Abe's routine, such as gardening, playing with water or sand, finger painting, and finding objects in tactile boxes. These activities gave Abe the needed tactile input and reduced his sensory-seeking behaviors.
- If Abe still displayed those behaviors, he was shown a STOP sign and redirected to one of the mentioned tactile activities.
- During stressful activities, Abe had scheduled calm breaks to avoid overwhelming him. His parents and teachers monitored him for signs of stress and moved him to a quiet area if needed.
- To help Abe with having his hair cut, he was given a head massage before, and during the cut, he used a weighted cushion and was given a tactile activity to do. His mother cut his hair at home once a week to help him get used to the sensation in a familiar space, and the recurrence of the activity helped him tolerate it more progressively.
- To help with his dentist appointments, Abe was shown photographs as visual examples of what

would happen and what was expected from him. As a positive reinforcement, he would be allowed to play with water when he allowed the dentist to examine him.

- Lastly, his parents and teachers started using visual communication strategies to facilitate Abe's understanding. These included photographs, transition cards, choice boards, and visual depictions of structured activities.

Isaiah's Story

Isaiah is 16 years old, and he has autism, ADHD, and a severe learning disability. His parents and teachers have reported aggressive outbursts and episodes in school transportation and in class, as well as some self-care and hygiene issues.

Isaiah has been shouting, covering his ears, and occasionally hitting when faced with activities and situations he does not enjoy, in response to noise, and as a response to showering or cutting his nails and hair. He has difficulties focusing on school tasks, especially if he has to work alone, and shows signs of anxiety in new activities or environments.

After being assessed by healthcare professionals, they concluded that Isaiah has problems processing and regulating sensory input:

- Isaiah's difficulty in tolerating classes and his inability to remain focused were caused by a sensitivity to noise. In addition, as he tends to be very vigilant of his surroundings, he would get distracted by visual stimuli. His refusal to shower or cut his nails showed he is oversensitive to touch.

- Professionals found that Isaiah sought sensory stimuli, especially visual ones, and that he enjoyed deep pressure.

The professionals suggested the following strategies:

- Background noise should be reduced as much as possible. If not possible, Isaiah was given noise-cancelling headphones or earplugs.
- When presented with an intensive task in a noisy environment, Isaiah should be given regular breaks or be moved to a calmer space.
- When overstimulated, Isaiah can make noise himself or cover his ears to let parents and teachers know. This would allow them to use one of the mentioned strategies and try to prevent a meltdown.
- Parents and teachers reduced visual clutter and used visual markers to define work areas and limit distractions.
- To help with anxiety, Isaiah started using weighted items, swimming, and carrying objects that provided some pressure.
- Activities related to hygiene were scheduled and communicated through visuals to help reduce his anxiety. His parents and caregivers were instructed to use a heavy touch and to try to make the activities as short as possible. Weighted items were used during these times to help Isaiah stay calm,

and he was scheduled to do an enjoyable activity afterward.

SENSORY ACTIVITIES FOR AUTISTIC CHILDREN

Autistic children can benefit greatly from sensory activities, as these can help them regulate their sensory input and work on their sensory skills. This way, children can learn to identify and process sensory information in a safe environment.

Studies have shown that these activities can improve communication and social interaction for children with ASD, help with relaxation, and reduce their stress levels, improving their mood and behavior.

Sensory activities are usually also part of a broader therapy plan (e.g., sensory integration therapy) to develop the child's ability to process and respond to stimuli. The incorporation of these activities into their daily routine helps their parents and caregivers support the development of the child's skills.

Given the proven benefits of sensory activities, they should be considered an essential part of any therapeutic plan for ASD.

Best Sensory Activities for Autistic Children

There are countless types of beneficial sensory activities, but here are some common examples:

- **Sensory bins:** A bin filled with materials such as sand, beans, rice, or small toys and objects can help with fine motor skills and hand-eye coordination.
- **Play dough:** The tactile nature of this activity provides sensory input and helps with both motor skills and hand-eye coordination.
- **Sensory bottles:** Filling a bottle with beads, glitter, water, or other small objects can help provide children with tactile and visual stimulation.
- **Swings:** The swinging motion can help with balance and coordination, provide sensory input, and help with calm and relaxation.
- **Bubble wrap:** Popping bubble wrap isn't only a fun activity but can also be calming and provide sensory input.
- **Water play:** A bin with water and small toys and objects helps with coordination and can be a calming activity.
- **Trampolines:** The bouncing motion can help the child to practice their balance and coordination.
- **Painting with shaving cream:** By playing with shaving cream on a window, a mirror, or other surfaces, the child can explore the texture and draw shapes and letters, practicing fine motor skills, coordination, and creativity. This activity should be supervised to ensure that the child doesn't ingest any shaving cream.
- **Sensory walks:** Creating a path for the child to walk or crawl along using textured materials can provide tactile stimulation.
- **Pouring station:** By pouring materials like sand, rice, or water from one container to another,

children can work on their coordination and fine
motor skills.

- **Ball pit:** Ball pits can provide a calming space to
  relax or a place to safely jump and dive.
- **Plastic bag kites:** Constructing and flying a kite
  can help with creativity, motor skills, and
  coordination and can be an enjoyable and calming
  activity.
- **Sensory play mats:** A mat with varied textures and
  objects is a good way to provide tactile stimulation.

Outdoor Sensory Activities

Doing outdoor activities not only helps with sensory stimulation but also gives the children the opportunity to socialize
with peers and enjoy nature. For children who struggle with
traditional sports, outdoor activities are a good way to exercise and develop their motor skills.

Here are some sensory activities you can do outside of the
sensory room:

- **Nature walks:** A walk can be a great opportunity
  for your child to exercise and enjoy nature while
  still exploring textures, sounds, and colors.
- **Water play:** A sprinkle, a hose, or a kiddie pool are
  ways to translate water play to an outdoor setting.
- **Sand play:** A sandbox can be a great tactile
  experience, and small toys can help with
  coordination and motor skills.

- **Chalk art:** Drawing on the pavement is a great way to exercise creativity and provide tactile stimulation.
- **Obstacle course:** An obstacle course is a good way to combine sensory activities and textures.

Sensory Activities and Emotional Regulation

Many autistic children struggle with emotional regulation. Sensory activities can be an effective way to develop the skills needed to manage their emotions.

- **Deep pressure:** Deep pressure can help autistic children feel grounded and calm. This can be achieved with hugs, weighted blankets or vests, or with a therapy ball.
- **Breathing exercises:** Breathing exercises can help to reduce stress and anxiety. Teaching your children to take deep breaths during sensory play can help them with learning to regulate their emotions.
- **Music therapy:** Music has a big impact on emotions. Calming music can be a helpful tool during sensory play.
- **Calming scents:** If your child is not hypersensitive to scents, aromatherapy can help with creating a relaxing space.
- **Yoga:** Yoga is known to promote relaxation and reduce stress. You can introduce some simple poses in your child's routine as a way to help them regulate their emotions.

For autistic people, sensory processing issues can cause them to be overwhelmed in environments that are too loud, too bright, or that just have the wrong textures, scents, or colors. Providing them with spaces where they can relax their senses, experiment with textures and objects, and learn to emotionally regulate is key to helping them develop their skills.

CHAPTER 4

THE COMFORT OF PREDICTABILITY

No two autistic experiences are alike. Each journey and story is personal and has its own struggles, but there are some challenges that all persons on the spectrum share. The predictability and structure of a set routine can help by providing order and easing anxieties when faced with stressful and uncertain situations.

THE BENEFITS OF ROUTINES

All children thrive on routine, but for autistic children, predictability and the use of patterns play an even more significant role in their development and well-being. Establishing routines and adhering to them can profoundly impact several aspects of their lives, fostering their independence and supporting their social and emotional growth. These are some of the benefits that routine can offer:

- **Reduce stress and power struggles:** Routines provide a sense of familiarity and predictability, which in turn reduces anxiety and stress for autistic children. By knowing what to expect in different situations, such as during transitions or daily activities, they feel more secure and confident. This familiarity minimizes the likelihood of power struggles and meltdowns, as they can navigate through their day with greater ease and self-assurance.

- **Improve cooperation and motivation:** A structured and predictable environment promotes a sense of safety and security, enabling children to feel more at ease and receptive to learning and engagement. With reduced stress levels, they are more likely to cooperate with caregivers and educators, facilitating the practice of existing skills and the introduction of new ones. By creating a less stressful atmosphere, routines enhance motivation and willingness to participate in various activities and tasks.

- **Create an environment of security and comfort:** Consistent routines create a stable and secure environment for autistic children, minimizing the unpredictability of new sounds, behaviors, or events. This sense of security fosters a feeling of comfort and stability, enabling them to navigate their surroundings with confidence and ease. By reducing the number of new stimuli, routines help regulate sensory experiences, promoting a calmer and more regulated emotional state.

- **Prompt a genuine sense of ownership over their day:** Routines empower autistic children by providing a clear framework for their daily activities and responsibilities. By knowing what tasks lie ahead, they can develop a sense of ownership over their day, taking pride in their accomplishments and progress. This increased sense of control and autonomy fosters self-esteem and self-confidence, laying the foundation for greater independence and self-advocacy.

- **Build stronger caregiver-child connections:** Consistent routines not only benefit autistic children but also deepen the bond between caregivers and their children. By providing a structured and supportive environment, routines promote feelings of security and trust, strengthening the emotional connection between parent and child. This sense of safety and predictability nurtures positive interactions and communication, fostering a nurturing and supportive relationship.
- **Help with learning:** Familiarity and predictability are essential elements for effective learning, especially for autistic children who may struggle with transitions and unfamiliar environments. Routines create a stable and comfortable backdrop for learning, allowing children to focus their attention and energy on acquiring new skills and knowledge. By minimizing distractions and anxiety-provoking stimuli, routines optimize the learning environment, promoting engagement and success.

Thomas's Story

Thomas is six years old, and he was diagnosed with severe autism at the age of three. He is semi-verbal and has acquired gross motor skills, but his fine motor skills are severely lacking. He needs significant support in his day-to-day activities at home and at school. The demands of his daily tasks seem to be a cause of anxiety for Thomas.

As part of a study, researchers examine Thomas's routine to better understand how he copes with anxiety. They found that Thomas has developed resilience strategies for most of his daily tasks, such as biting his toothbrush when freshening up in the morning, delaying getting clothed to avoid the travel to school, making a mess when eating if his caregivers were upset with him, and singing if he had to be on the bus, among others. In general, they deducted that Thomas coped with anxiety by exhibiting challenging behaviors, expressing his preferences through actions rather than language, repeating actions and phrases that had impacted him, using sensory tools that he had selected, and ignoring teachers and caregivers.

The researchers found that Thomas was more likely to cooperate in those instances where a routine or behavior was not imposed on him, such as his teachers allowing him to settle on his own when entering the classroom, being allowed to eat using only one hand, or sleeping with his lights on. They concluded that his resilience strategies were a reaction to anxiety and that his chosen routine should not be disturbed. In those cases where he coped through aggressive behavior, the teachers and caregivers should take into account that these behaviors stemmed from stress and anxiety and respond accordingly.

HOW TO CREATE A DAILY ROUTINE

The routine of an autistic child should be structured and organized around their daily needs and their natural order. Having a visual reminder of their daily routine can help them establish and predict the rhythm of their day. Giving them the time to take in this schedule will also reduce any anxiety and provide them with a sense of stability.

In order to create your child's routine, you need to mix the necessary tasks with fun and engaging activities to create a balance between what they need to do and what they enjoy doing. Make sure to include their unique hobbies and interests when planning activities.

The following steps might be of assistance when creating a routine:

1. **Identify important tasks:** Start by outlining what you want your child to get done during the day, like chores, homework, meals, and any other task that is relevant for your family. Then, break these tasks into small, manageable steps. Remember that your routine should be predictable and specific, so lay out the steps and options clearly. If necessary, include detailed instructions for each step.
2. **Create a schedule:** Organize all the identified tasks and their instructions in a schedule, including keywords and visual aids such as images, photos, and videos. Use timers and alarms to help with the transition between tasks.
3. **Refer to the schedule often:** When preparing for the day and during tasks refer to the schedule

constantly to let them know where they are and what comes next. Provide reinforcements with descriptive phrases (e.g., "Good job cleaning up your room!") to provide reassurance and instill confidence.

4. **Be consistent and flexible:** Consistency is key when following a routine, so make sure to stick to it. However, allow yourself and your child some flexibility while also preparing for changes in advance to avoid upsetting them.

Tips to Successfully Maintain a Routine

Consistency and practice are essential for adopting and maintaining a routine. There might be struggles in the beginning, but sticking to it and providing positive reinforcement will help your child to settle. You can also:

- Praise your child for following the routine.
- Give visual aids and create lists that can be marked or crossed off.
- Use timers and alarms.
- Include choices to help your child feel more in control.
- Encourage consistency but allow for flexibility. You can have a visual schedule that allows for tasks to be rearranged so you can include new steps or changes in the schedule and go over them with your child.

Cathy's Story

Cathy is a sophomore in college and she is autistic. She lives in her college dorm, which has shared bathrooms. Cathy has found that, for her, routine is most important during the school year. She likes to use a specific shower in the mornings and sit at a certain spot during classes.

On the days when her preferred shower is already taken, or someone has occupied her spot in class, she gets frustrated and feels that the rhythm of her day has been interrupted. Depending on her mood, her reaction to these changes in routine might vary from annoyance to a full meltdown.

COPING WITH UNEXPECTED CHANGES

Children with ASD might respond in different ways to changes, from socially withdrawing to tantrums or even meltdowns or aggressive behavior. It is important to remember that these reactions are motivated by stress, anxiety, and, sometimes, the inability to properly communicate their feelings and emotions.

While unexpected situations sometimes imply big changes (e.g., a change in school or neighborhood), the routine of an autistic person can be shaken by the smallest alterations, like leaving the house slightly earlier than normal or forgetting to cut the annoying tag of a new shirt.

Not all stressful situations can be planned for in advance, so it is important to not only prepare your children for upcoming changes and events but also to prepare tools and calming exercises for a possible unexpected situation.

How to Prepare Children for Changes in Routine

Supporting your child through changes in their routine, either unexpected or planned, will require empathy, patience, and a few strategies to help them navigate situations that might seem simple but can give a sense of uncertainty:

- **Visual schedules and timers** are a clear way to show your child what is happening and when, both for a daily routine and for an unexpected upcoming event. Having a visual aid that is used specifically for unplanned events can help your child be more open to surprises and unforeseen circumstances.

- In the same vein, **picture cards** of daily events and tasks can help to explain a change and place it in an already existing schedule. It can be helpful to have a schedule or routine board that can be rearranged. Even if your child is used to a set routine, having the ability to make changes gives you the opportunity to introduce a little bit of flexibility in their day-to-day.

- Introducing **new interesting activities** in a set routine can show your children that a change can be positive and fun. You can plan activities that align with their interests so they have an extra reason to welcome the change or do a calming and relaxing activity to reduce any anxiety that might arise from the deviation from the routine.

- A **countdown calendar** that your children can keep track of can help reduce the stress of an upcoming event. Being aware of a change in schedule a few

days in advance can give your child the possibility
to adjust to the event, know what is going to
happen, and process any emotions or feelings that
this change may provoke.

- A **video** about a new event or place can help reduce
  your child's anxiety by making them familiar with
  those situations.
- **Social stories** (short narrations about situations
  and activities that include pictures) are a good way
  to prepare your child for stressful events like going
  to the dentist. These stories describe the possible
  reasons for events, how the situation will unfold,
  who will be there, and what is expected of the
  participants.

How to Help Children With Unexpected Changes

- Have a **picture card for unexpected events** (it
  could say "surprise" or "?"). Use it for both negative
  and positive events to avoid your child giving a
  negative connotation to surprises.
- Allow for **extra time to adjust** if you know your
  child will react negatively to the change. Some
  children might struggle more than others with
  unexpected changes, so let your child process their
  feelings at their own pace.
- Try to redirect your child to a **calming activity**
  where they can relax and regulate their emotions.
  Reading, engaging in activities that involve
  creativity, doing breathing exercises, or any other
  soothing activity that your child enjoys can work as
  an outlet for their frustration and anxiety.

- **Validate your child's feelings** in a calm manner. Acknowledge what they are feeling without judgment or dismissal, and let them know that it's normal to feel apprehensive or scared during a transition. By validating their experience, you can help them foster a sense of security and trust and build up their confidence in their resilience.

For autistic children, routine and predictability are a source of order and security in a world that can feel loud and chaotic. Knowing what to do in advance gives them control over the situation and helps them manage their emotions and expectations. However, deviating from the familiar schedule due to unexpected events can be a source of great stress and anxiety, so it is important to not only help them prepare for upcoming changes but also give them tools to emotionally regulate and adapt to surprising situations.

CHAPTER 5
MELTDOWNS

Jenny's Story

Jenny is five years old, and she has mild autism. She is completely verbal, has little issues socializing, and is completely integrated into her kindergarten classroom. She recently has been having meltdowns when it is time to enter school, screaming, crying, and running away from her teachers.

Her parents are concerned because they have not been able to identify a possible trigger, especially since Jenny has been schooled for two years already and has never behaved like this, and there haven't been any changes to her routine.

UNDERSTANDING MELTDOWNS

It is very difficult for non-autistic people to understand what a meltdown feels like, especially when the majority of studies have researched meltdowns from the parents' and caregivers' point of view. Just recently have researchers started to approach the subject from the perspective of those having the meltdown to try to understand their feelings and experiences.

Most autistic people have described meltdowns as being overwhelmed by sensory information but also by emotional and social stress. Their emotions feel extremely heightened, to the point where they experience problems thinking and remembering things. They struggle with staying in control, describing the meltdown as a release of pent-up emotions and frustrations.

While an autistic adult might sometimes have an easier time controlling their meltdowns and identifying and avoiding potential triggers, this is much more difficult for autistic children and teenagers. As they are still learning to regulate their emotions, they are more likely to feel overwhelmed and lose control of their behavior.

It is important to remember that not all meltdowns look the same; they might include behaviors like crying, rocking, hitting, or withdrawing. No matter the behavior displayed, meltdowns are a sign of distress and can make it hard for children to participate in everyday activities.

Avoiding Meltdowns

In order to avoid meltdowns, autistic children and teenagers need to learn to identify the situations that they find difficult and will overwhelm them and what to do in these situations.

- **Identifying difficult situations:** What constitutes a difficult situation varies according to the person.

You can help your child to make a list of potentially triggering situations so they can practice being aware of them. As meltdowns can also be caused by stress or by an accumulation of small events, keeping a record of past meltdowns and their causes can be helpful.

- **Noticing early signs:** It is important for your child to learn to recognize when they are feeling uncomfortable or overwhelmed. You can help them by discussing the emotions that might lead to a meltdown, like anxiety or fear, and making them describe the physical feelings of a meltdown.

- **Developing coping strategies:** There are several things your child can do to remain as calm as possible, such as breathing exercises, muscle relaxation techniques, or just taking a break and listening to music. If they are being triggered by a noisy environment, they can go somewhere quieter or less crowded. They can also use sensory aids like headphones to avoid specific triggers.

- **Practicing coping strategies:** In order for your child to remember and use these strategies when they are overwhelmed, they need to practice them while feeling calm. It can be helpful to add them to their routine, so they become familiar with and discuss practical actions and sensory aids with teachers and other caregivers.

Leading Up to a Meltdown

If you sense your child is stressed or overwhelmed, these are some things you can do to help them calm down:

1. Identify the signs of your child being overwhelmed.
2. See what elements of their environment can be modified to help them relax (e.g., dimming the lights, turning down the music).
3. Offer your child a few choices of calming activities to redirect their emotions. This could be something as simple as going on a walk, changing their current activity, or doing an errand.
4. Provide them with their sensory aids if needed, and remind them to use the relaxation techniques they have learned. Remain calm, try not to say much, and give them space.

During a Meltdown

If the meltdown is unavoidable:

1. Guide your child to a place where they can feel safe and protected. If possible, try to find a secluded place so they can express their emotions without fear of judgment or interference.
2. Touch them as little as possible, give them space, and make others stay out of the way. Encourage other people to respect your child's boundaries to avoid overwhelming them further.
3. In order to mitigate sensory overload, try to reduce environmental stimuli as much as possible.

Dimming the lights, lowering noise levels, and providing sensory aids such as headphones, earplugs, or a weighted blanket can create a more soothing atmosphere and help with relaxation.

4. Communicate with your child in a calm manner, using gentle words and a soothing tone of voice to help them through their distress. If they don't want to talk, your presence alone can serve as support and offer comfort, stability, and a sense of safety.

5. Be patient and understanding as you wait for them to relax and ease out of the meltdown. Don't rush or pressure them, as it could exacerbate their distress.

After a Meltdown

After coming down from a meltdown, your child will most likely feel tired and sometimes embarrassed. If possible, a calming activity is a good way to help them relax. After they have calmed down, it is helpful to discuss what happened, what triggered the meltdown, and what emotions they experienced. This will help them recognize their emotions and also avoid future triggers.

If your child has recurrent meltdowns and you are unable to manage them, you can consult your child's doctor and other healthcare professionals to discuss possible strategies and therapies to help.

Sam's Story

Sam is the mother of an autistic six-year-old son. With her partner, they have decided to homeschool their son, and they prefer not to use punishment as a form of discipline. They are looking for a child's psychologist in order to get a formal evaluation and diagnosis.

Sam and her partner had a meeting with a recommended professional, where they told her about their son and their preferred parenting style. The psychologist strongly suggested a more disciplinary approach and expressed her beliefs that they should not only encourage their son to go to school and socialize more but that they should force him to do it to help him overcome his fears.

In the end, Sam and her partner declined her services and continued looking for a professional who would be a better fit for their family. They believe that forcing their child to be independent would be counterintuitive, as they know he would work better at his own pace and, when he feels confident enough, he will take those steps on his own.

Sam prefers a gentle approach when faced with a meltdown, trying to empathize with her son and listening to his fears and emotions without judgment. She makes sure that her son feels loved and secure, even if his distress prevents him from hearing her talk, and that he knows that he will never be punished for being overwhelmed. She has a few sensory aids at hand, should he ever need them, and once he is calmer, they practice calming strategies together.

MELTDOWNS VS. TANTRUMS

Autistic meltdowns can be easily confused with a temper tantrum, as they include cries, sobs, and yells, but meltdowns are more extreme and can result in a person injuring themselves, destroying things, and even running away.

Temper tantrums are common among toddlers and young children, and they are often a manipulation tactic to get something they want. They are usually resolved when the child gets what they wanted.

In contrast, an autistic meltdown is involuntary and is a response to sensory or emotional overload, which leads the person to feel overwhelmed. Meltdowns can occur no matter the age and they resolve on their own once the person is able to calm down. Still, during the aftermath of a meltdown, the person will need time and space to regulate their emotions, and they might not be able to fully recall the episode.

Autistic children can also have temper tantrums, so it is very important to be able to differentiate them from meltdowns, as the approach to each situation is different. Tantrums are goal-oriented, so most of the time they will arise from an unmet or denied request. Unlike meltdowns, tantrums are not preceded by signs of distress, and they are intended for the attention of parents or other adults.

PARENTS' DO'S AND DON'TS FOR MELTDOWNS

What to Do

- Keep calm. Your child will need your help, so make sure to take deep breaths and focus on them.
- Look for a quiet area where your child can feel safe. If possible, dim the lights and reduce the noise as much as possible. You can even have a designated "calm area" in your house.
- Offer support and comfort through words, hugs, and touches if your child is ok with it.
- Let your child know that it's ok to feel overwhelmed and that you understand they are having a hard time.
- After the meltdown, work with your child to help them feel better. This could be with breathing exercises, using a sensory toy, or doing a calming activity. Helping them cope with their emotions will make future meltdowns easier to manage.

What to Avoid

- Don't raise your voice or punish your child. Remember that meltdowns are involuntary and that your child has no control over them. Instead, focus on supporting them.
- Don't force them to talk about their feelings or emotions. Once they feel better, you can see if they are open to having a conversation.

- Don't ask them too many questions. Keep your words simple and clear.
- Don't ignore your child's needs. If you think that the meltdown is a result of your child needing something like rest or food, take care of it as soon as possible.

I recall one time when we were in J.C. Penney. My daughter Lizzie must've been seven or eight. She was acting up and making a lot of noise. At the time, I thought she was just throwing a tantrum, but looking back, I know it was an autism meltdown. In fact, this may have been one of the first big signs she had autism, and I missed it.

She had gotten very focused on one item in the store, but it was time to move on. This wasn't as simple as a young child hearing, "No, we can't buy that today," and throwing a tantrum. When she was that young, she would hyperfocus on shelves in stores and rearrange them. In this case, that's what she was doing when it was time to move on to continue shopping. I carried her out of the store, and I didn't look at anybody or anything but the door. I rushed her to the car so she wouldn't disturb anybody else in the store.

I didn't recognize the signs of her meltdown at the time, and there were not many easy ways to handle them. If you're like me, introverted, and do not want anyone to notice you, when these happen in public, it can be pretty embarrassing. Just breathe and be there for your child. If you get frustrated and tense, your child can feel that. Doing so will only make the situation worse. Make sure your child is safe, and make sure they know that. Reassure them and let them know they're okay.

MELTDOWNS VS. SHUTDOWNS AND WHY SHUTDOWNS HAPPEN

Autistic Shutdowns

A shutdown is the result of being overwhelmed and having low energy. If an autistic person shuts down, it usually means they are past the point of trying to calm down or battle through the stress. Shutting down is the body's way of trying to conserve energy. In comparison to meltdowns, shutdowns are a muted response to stress, which makes them more difficult to spot.

If an autistic shutdown prolongs in time, it can turn into burnout.

Signs of Autistic Shutdowns

There are a few signs of an autistic shutdown:

- Being completely silent and unable to communicate in any way.
- Withdrawing to a quiet space to avoid the cause of the shutdown.
- Being unable to move from where they are.
- Lying down completely still.
- Staring into space or dissociating (staring into nothingness while sitting or standing).

It is important to remember that all behavior is communication. If they are covering their ears or their face, closing their eyes, or blinking a lot, these are all signs. They might be reacting to your voice tone, they might be dizzy, or wanting to avoid eye contact.

Social Struggles During Autistic Shutdown

Leading up to or during a shutdown, autistic people might struggle to make sense. They will have difficulty talking or typing, and they may trip with their words, which can cause them to become frustrated with themselves. Yawning, stuttering, having speech errors, or directly not speaking may also happen.

Is Autistic Burnout a Type of Depression?

Though depression might share some of its symptoms with prolonged burnout, they are different. Depression typically revolves around feelings of helplessness and despair, which are not common with autistic burnout, which is characterized by exhaustion, loss of function, and low tolerance to stimulus.

Their symptoms overlap when it comes to socialization, executive functioning, emotions, fatigue, motivation, and concentration, which can lead to confusion and misdiagnosis.

Recovering From an Autistic Shutdown

The purpose of the body when shutting down is to conserve energy. Due to the way they are socialized, autistic children might not avoid doing things before or after a shutdown, even if they are overwhelmed or still recovering.

As a parent, it is important to remind your child that breaks are needed and that they don't need to forgo their boundaries for the sake of others. You can also help them by reducing their obligations, scheduling time off, and allowing them to have alone time.

How to Help Autistic Shutdowns

- Encourage your child to rest. Allow them to retire somewhere quiet and comfortable where they can be undisturbed. Providing them with a weighted blanket can offer a sense of comfort and security, alleviate anxiety, and help with relaxation.
- Reduce the number of people around them and create a calm environment with low stimulation. If your child does not want to interact with others, respect their needs and explain to others the importance of giving them space.
- Support any self-regulatory behavior they might engage in. Allow them to stim if they need to, and encourage them to do any activity that they might find soothing, such as listening to music or reading.
- Encourage them to do comforting and relaxing activities to help them unwind. Prepare them a warm bath or shower, offer them familiar objects such as a favorite toy or blanket, or bring them their preferred snacks.

Emi's Story

Emi is autistic. When she feels extremely overwhelmed, she doesn't usually have meltdowns, but she tends to shut down. For her, shutdowns can last for days, especially those caused by stress and emotional overload.

She doesn't like talking or moving much during shutdowns. While her body is shutting down due to stress, she still feels the sensory input that led her to become overwhelmed.

CULTIVATING PATIENCE WITH YOUR AUTISTIC CHILD

Being a parent of an autistic child requires patience and love. And while affection comes naturally, patience requires practice and time to develop. Communication issues and health struggles can make parenting an autistic child emotionally, physically, and mentally exhausting, but there are some things that can help you cultivate your patience:

- **Remember to remain calm:** The repetitive behaviors, strict routines, and having to reiterate instructions can be stress-inducing and result in outbursts. Take a step back, breathe deeply, and remember to stay calm to better help your child.
- **Look at things from your child's perspective:** Put yourself in your child's shoes and try to empathize with their struggles. Ask yourself why they might be acting that way and try to come up with a response to help better their behavior.
- **Ask for support:** If you are overwhelmed or need help, ask for it. Develop a support network around you that can assist you when you need it.
- **Break big hurdles down into small steps:** Tackle your problems step by step and work your way up to the bigger things.
- **Focus on the positive:** Good mood and behavior are contagious, so focus on the good things.
- **Do something else that is relaxing:** Don't wait until you are at your limit to take time to relax and unwind.
- **Seek momentary refuge:** During meltdowns and shutdowns, you might also need to remove yourself

from the situation, so do it if you need it to avoid a meltdown of your own.

- **Consider respite care** *(see Chapter 10):* If you are particularly worn down, consider leaving your child with a trusted caregiver and focus on your mental and physical health so you can better help them.

Meltdowns and shutdowns are the result of being stressed and overwhelmed. They take a huge toll on autistic persons, but also on their parents and caregivers. It is important, then, to be attentive to the signs of distress and exhaustion and to be patient with your child while also taking care of your own well-being.

CHAPTER 6
EMOTIONS, EMPATHY, AND REPETITIVE BEHAVIORS

Will's Story

Will is the parent of a four-year-old autistic boy who has been having trouble managing his emotions. Will started talking to him about recognizing and acknowledging emotions, describing how they make him feel, and naming them.

Will knows that it is important for him as a parent to lead by example, so he makes a point of talking about his emotions and explaining them to his child, admitting that he also struggles sometimes. He makes sure to encourage his son when he talks about his emotions, and he doesn't aim to solve the emotions but to discuss them.

CONNECTING WITH EMOTIONS

Maria's Story

Maria has two autistic children. As a parent to someone with a disability, she has to be flexible in her expectations and look for clues in their expressions. She knows the tells of their different emotions, which stims they use depending on their mood, and what sensory toys they prefer. She knows that these ways of expressing emotion help her children to be more confident in themselves and with others.

These are some of the strategies she suggests for helping autistic children express their emotions:

- **Observe their facial expressions, behavior, and play:** When children lack the words to express their feelings, these feelings manifest in other ways. Look for clues in their body language, and ask follow-up questions to make sure you are interpreting them correctly.
- **Watch how you express and react to emotions:** Your children are going to watch and imitate the way you act. If there are feelings that you consider unacceptable or don't express, they can feel that certain emotions should not be displayed.
- **Teach your child about the different emotions and how they can be felt:** This can be done with cards and visual cues followed up with questions about their own experiences.

EMOTIONAL SELF-REGULATION

Jeremy has an autistic son. One day his son had a meltdown, one of the worst they could remember. He was crying, running, shaking, and was clearly struggling to regulate his emotions. Trying to help him and wondering what had been the trigger, Jeremy realized he had forgotten to put socks on his son after the shower. The little child loved wearing socks, so after putting them on he calmed down, watched TV, and then was ready to go to bed.

In this case, socks were a way for him to regulate his emotions, but sometimes it can be a challenging thing to do.

What is Emotional Regulation?

Emotional regulation is the ability to manage and respond to an emotional experience. This can mean a lot of things, from something as easy as putting on a pair of socks, to therapy, counseling, or other coping strategies.

Emotional regulation is very personal and might not always work, so it can be challenging for the parents of an autistic child, as they are more prone to emotional struggles due to their sensitivities.

Importance of Emotional Regulation Skills

Emotional regulation is key for attaining a better quality of life, as it can lead to fewer outbursts and help decrease anxiety. They can help soothe situations that might lead to frustration, anger, and meltdowns.

In order to learn to regulate emotions, children need to understand what causes them, both positive and negative emotions. From there, emotional regulation skills can be used to turn negative emotions into positive ones.

How to Help With Emotional Regulation

- **Practicing deep breathing exercises:** Taking deep breaths is a common exercise used to calm down, and can be easily taught to children as a first step if they are feeling overwhelmed.
- **Establishing zones of regulation:** It can be helpful to have a system to help your child recognize if they are in need of emotional regulation. You can use a color-coded system, a numerical system, or a system of emotional levels. This way, they have a practical way to assess where they're at emotionally.
- **Discussing reactions:** Once your child is able to recognize emotions and their levels, you can discuss with them how they would react and which reactions are appropriate according to the situation and place. If needed, you can suggest alternative responses. Providing your child with nonjudgmental feedback can help them self-reflect on their behaviors and make better decisions.
- **Exemplifying appropriate behavior:** In order for your child to react appropriately, you have to do the same. If you are able to cope with and handle your own emotions, they'll have a model of what to do.
- **Communicating expectations:** Children will copy your communication the same way they do your behaviors. If you calmly explain what is expected of

them, they will be more likely to recognize situations and apply the skills learned.

- **Acknowledging their feelings:** Many times, children need someone to know how they are feeling before trying to regulate their emotions. Acknowledging they are frustrated, upset, or angry can help them recognize these emotions and work through them.
- **Practicing calming activities:** There are many skills that can help with self-regulation. Help your child find the ones best suited to them, such as gadgets or counting strategies.
- **Having a calming space:** You can have a designated space at home that is comforting and will help them to calm down and practice their skills.
- **Taking a break:** Sometimes, all the child needs is to step away from a situation. Help them recognize when they should do this and what the best way to do it is.
- **Exercising:** Physical exercise can help with working through emotions. If your child enjoys exercising, encourage them to do it if they are feeling emotionally dysregulated.
- **Solving problems together:** Talk with your child to see if emotional dysregulation is causing personal problems, and discuss possible ways to solve them.
- **Helping them boost their mood:** Discuss likes and dislikes and what makes them happy or sad, so you have ways to help them boost their mood.

- **Setting small tasks:** Big tasks can be overwhelming. Divide tasks and chores into small, manageable steps that they can tackle easily.
- **Detecting emotional triggers:** Knowing what can possibly trigger your child can help them understand the causes of complex negative emotions.
- **Practicing words:** For autistic children who are verbal, being able to name and describe emotions is a big part of emotionally regulating themselves. If your child is nonverbal, you can help them use other forms of communication, like cards, sign language, or an electronic device.
- **Deep pressure:** Using deep pressure can provide a sense of safety and security when your child is emotionally overwhelmed.
- **Reassurance:** If they are feeling emotionally dysregulated, your child might feel like emotions are impossible to overcome. Reassure them that this is not the case and that these feelings will pass.
- **Having a routine:** See if their routine has been thrown off and help them get back on track.
- **Offering food and drinks:** Even if hunger and thirst might not be the lead cause of their dysregulation, a snack or drink can help them focus on managing their emotions.
- **Giving them choices:** Having a choice can allow the child to feel in control of a situation, but you need to be careful, as sometimes choice can be overwhelming.

RECOGNIZING EMOTIONS IN OTHERS

Children are usually able to recognize basic facial expressions when they are around four months old, and they can reciprocate those emotions around the seven-month-old mark. Being unable to do this is a common early sign of autism, as people on the spectrum tend to have difficulties identifying and recognizing emotions, facial expressions, body language, and voice tonality.

While recognizing and interpreting emotions is challenging for autistic persons, it is not impossible. These are some steps that can help your children to learn how to recognize and label emotions:

1. Choose age-appropriate activities that teach emotions and that correspond with their strengths and developmental level.
2. Focus on one emotion at a time and take small steps. Start with the most basic emotions and move on as they are able to identify them.
3. Use visual cards and pictures to help your child recognize each emotion and the parts of the face that are involved in displaying it.
4. Make learning about emotions fun and engaging through the use of cartoons, pantomimes, and drawings.
5. Use a variety of activities and visuals so they can practice emotion recognition in different people.
6. Use visual stories and children's books to help your child label different emotions in the context of a story.

7. Make them apply their knowledge in places like the playground or the doctor's office. This will help them generalize emotions.
8. Ask your child to name emotions to strengthen the connection between the word and the emotional status and expression.

EMPATHY

Phil's Story

Phil is 27 years old, and he is autistic. He always found emotions challenging to interpret, and even though he has learned to identify them by facial expressions and body language, he still struggles with the social cues and context related to them.

His work entails a great deal of talking to customers, so he has practiced deciphering how others are feeling, but he feels that some people might display emotions that aren't genuine in order to benefit from him. In the end, he has decided not to worry about that and treat everybody according to the emotions they openly display, as he'd rather empathize with others than doubt their motives.

Autism and Empathy

To be empathic is to be able to understand and share the feelings of others. Autistic people may have trouble reading the body language and non-verbal cues that communicate emotion and understanding language that is not literal, like sarcasm, metaphors, and double meanings.

This might lead to the belief that people on the spectrum are emotionless, which is not true. These problems are a misreading issue, which causes miscommunication. Once autistic people understand what is being conveyed, they are able to empathize with others and put themselves in their shoes.

Autism and Social Cues

Social cues are a big part of social communication, and they come in various forms, like voice tones, expressions, body language, and keywords. They are usually learned at an early age, but they are challenging for people with ASD.

Studies have shown that brain reactions to facial expressions differ in autistic and non-autistic persons and that people on the spectrum might place more importance on direct communication, such as verbal language or direct eye contact.

The Outlook

Autism is a complex disorder, but this does not mean these communication issues are insurmountable. There are a multitude of resources and interventions that can aid an autistic person in developing their social skills and their participation in their communities.

How to Develop Your Child's Empathy

- Attach empathy to behaviors: Empathy cannot always be seen, so attaching it to certain behaviors can be helpful. You can model these behaviors, explain them to your child, and use positive reinforcement when they use them. The behaviors can be **verbal** (phrases such as "Are you ok?," "I'm sorry that happened," "How can I help you?"), be related to **intonation**, **facial expressions** (not smiling when someone is hurting, clapping when someone does something right), **appropriate gestures** (hugging, patting someone's back), and **spontaneous behaviors** (when your child behaves empathetically on their own, reinforce it).

- Positive reinforcement: A behavior that is followed by a stimulus is more likely to reoccur. You can reinforce behavior through verbal praise or a reward such as candy, a preferred snack, or extra playtime.
- Role-play with toys: Using dolls or toys, present a scenario and use the toys to model an appropriate empathetic response. You can use these scenarios as a reference when situations happen in real life.
- Modeling and prompting: Studies have shown that modeling behavior and prompting your child to engage in this behavior is an effective way of teaching empathy. Use daily situations such as losing toys or doing chores to model an empathetic behavior and explain it to your child.
- Contrive situations with siblings/peers/parents: Create a situation where an empathetic response is needed, and prompt your child to respond correctly so they can practice the learned behaviors.

REPETITIVE AND RESTRICTIVE BEHAVIORS (RRBS)

One of the common traits of autistic individuals is repetitive and restrictive behaviors. Repetitive behaviors are those such as rocking the body or opening and closing doors and drawers over and over, while restrictive behaviors (also known as fixed interests) usually entail a high focus on an object, activity, or subject.

These behaviors are usually a way of calming oneself, and if they don't represent a threat to the person's wellbeing or a disruption to their routine, they don't necessarily need intervention.

Behaviors and Autism

These behaviors are listed in the *DSM-5* as one of autism's main traits and are described as obsessive, selective, unwavering, and without a purpose. Some specialists refer to them as "stereotypy" or "perseveration" due to the persistent repetition of acts, words, or phrases.

While adherence to routine is common in people with ASD, it is not enough to warrant an official diagnosis. The *DSM-5* observes that these behaviors have an abnormal intensity and focus and that their disruption causes extreme distress to the person. These behaviors usually manifest as:

- Stereotyped or repetitive motor movements, use of objects, or speech.
- Insistence on sameness, inflexible adherence to routines, or ritualized patterns of verbal or nonverbal behavior.

- Highly fixated interests that are atypical in intensity or focus.

What Stereotypy Behaviors Look Like

These behaviors and interests change from person to person. For some, it may be talking about the same subject over and over and knowing all the details about it. For others, it may be a constant physical movement that, in cases of severe autism, can be violent.

While some autistic persons engage in these behaviors constantly and others do it occasionally when they are upset, stressed, or anxious, all of them might have a stronger reaction than expected when asked to stop or change a behavior.

Some of these behaviors stand out because they are unusual for a non-autistic person, like prolonged rocking back and forth or obsessively turning a switch on and off, but in some people, they might not be so obvious. They might talk about an interest or recite a list that they recite often, which is only repetitive if you are close to them and have heard it before.

Are Repetitive Behaviors and Fixed Interests a Problem?

Repetitive behaviors are not exclusive to autism and can be found in most people in the form of nail-biting, tapping, pacing, or having a preferred show or topic. In milder cases of autism, these behaviors tend to be fairly unobtrusive and might even prove beneficial in their careers and activities. However, for some autistic people, they can present an

obstacle in their communication with the world and a distur-
bance to those around them.

Causes and Treatments

There are many theories about the origin of these behaviors
and interests, but so far, there has not been a definitive
answer. Most of these behaviors can be treated, but intervention is not always necessary, excluding those cases where
the behavior is dangerous or risky for the autistic person or
for others.

The treatments available to respond to the different theories
suggested, and their success, will depend on the individual:

- Behavioral therapy responds to the belief that these
  are behavioral issues and might implement
  techniques like rewards and consequences to
  diminish these behaviors.
- If you see repetitive behaviors as a self-calming
  response to sensory input, you can implement
  sensory integration techniques.
- If you believe that a fixation is the manifestation of
  a real interest, there are some therapies (like
  Floortime or Son-Rise) that can help develop those
  interests into activities.
- If you believe these behaviors are caused by a
  neurological issue or by anxiety, you can talk to
  your doctor to see if they can be managed with
  medication.

Jimmy's Story

Jimmy is an autistic 14-year-old. He prefers not to talk too much and does not enjoy socializing. His teachers observe that he displays disruptive repetitive behavior in school, especially vocalizing, hand flapping, and mouthing and that these behaviors only seem to subside when listening to music during his free time.

As part of a research study, Jimmy was first observed during a school day in different settings, such as the classroom, the cafeteria, and the hallways, and was allowed to listen to music while carrying on his activities.

During the next phase of the research, the music was stopped every time Jimmy was distracted, failed to answer a teacher, or deviated from the task at hand, and was only turned on once he resumed his activities. Though his academic performance improved with this method, he displayed more repetitive behaviors when the music was turned off.

The researchers came to the conclusion that Jimmy's repetitive behaviors were caused by a want for stimulation. When he was allowed to listen to music constantly, these behaviors subsided, but they appeared again when the music disappeared.

Charles's Story

Charles is a 13-year-old boy with autism. He presents an intellectual disability, but he has remarkable calendar calculation and musical abilities. His parents are looking for advice in order to optimize these interests.

When questioned by medical professionals, Charles indicated an interest in video games and YouTube videos. He recognized his abilities for calculation and music recognition, but he did not mention them when asked about his interests. He also showed a preoccupation with bettering his academic performance and being more independent as an adult and a dislike for the manual tasks he was assigned as part of his school program, which focused on trade job skills.

The researchers conducted a series of tests and psychological evaluations to determine Charles's capabilities and had a series of parental coaching sessions with his parents. The goal of these sessions was to help them understand their son's limitations and the importance of organizing pleasant activities that were centered around Charles's interests and not his strengths.

Charles attended a series of psychotherapy sessions in order to validate his feelings around his difficulties, give him emotional self-regulation tools, and make him understand what his possibilities were for education. He was moved to a school program that combined academic work with trade job skills in order to consider his interest in academic studies, no matter his intellectual limitations.

After a few months, the researchers made a follow-up assessment of Charles and found that his overall quality of life had increased. He was happier in his new class, and he was satisfied with the manual tasks assigned to him. He understood that pursuing a superior education was not realistic but that there were other programs and occupations possible. He was aware of his social and communication limitations but was more independent.

Autistic persons face many challenges when it comes to their feelings and emotions, recognizing them in other people, and managing their behaviors. While the issues are not usually risky or harmful, they are a barrier when it comes to socialization and relationships. It is important, then, to give them the tools necessary to overcome these hurdles in order to increase their communication skills and life quality.

CHAPTER 7
SOCIAL
COMMUNICATION

Social Communication

Autistic people are likely to enjoy activities with others as much as any other person. Nonetheless, social communication challenges are a big issue for those on the spectrum and are one of the main criteria for a diagnosis. While some people on the spectrum enjoy social interactions when initiated by others or might even initiate them themselves, many of them struggle with socializing despite a genuine desire for friendship.

Differences in socialization for autistic people might include:

- Struggling to respond, or not responding at all, to verbal communication.
- Using very few nonverbal gestures, such as nodding or hand gesturing.
- Struggling with eye contact.
- Having difficulty interpreting social cues or identifying them in other people's actions. Autistic

people will usually need these implied social rules to be explicitly taught and explained to them.

- Echoing words or patterns of words without any apparent meaning attached. Some autistic people are very good at mimicking as a way of fitting in socially.
- Struggling to communicate their needs or wants, which can lead to them becoming frustrated.
- Not sharing their interests with others or sharing them in a disproportionate manner without checking the other person's interest.

Predicting and Interpreting Others' Behavior

A crucial aspect of intellectual and social development is the ability to understand that other people have different needs, thoughts, and desires, a concept referred to in psychology as the "Theory of Mind." However, autistic individuals often find this fundamental aspect of human interaction to be challenging. This can significantly impact their ability to predict and interpret the behaviors of others, as well as understand how their own actions influence those around them.

For many people on the spectrum, recognizing and deciphering social cues is more of an intellectual process than an intuitive one. The nuances of social interactions (such as tone of voice, body language, or facial expressions) can be perplexing or even overwhelming. As a result, navigating social situations can feel like a complex puzzle with elusive and shifting rules.

However, socializing is a skill that can be learned and cultivated over time. With support and guidance, autistic individuals can learn to identify behaviors, navigate social contexts, and adapt to them accordingly.

Receptive and Expressive Communication

Receptive communication is the ability to understand other people's communicative attempts. This entails spoken language and all of its nuances, including language, facial expressions, and voice tones.

Autistic people have a tendency to understand verbal language literally, and they might struggle with the rhythm of conversations, which can lead to misunderstandings. When communicating with someone on the spectrum, it can be helpful to be aware of their tendency to concrete thinking. They might have difficulties understanding manners of speech, double meanings, and metaphors.

Expressive communication, which entails language and non-verbal behavior, can also vary in autistic people. Some may experience significant linguistic delays or be non-verbal. Others might have a well-developed language and vocabulary but express themselves in unusual ways.

People with ASD tend to particularly struggle with eye contact, finding it uncomfortable, rude, or even painful, which can lead to them appearing uninterested or impolite.

Spoken Language Development

Some autistic people never develop their spoken language and resort to other ways of communication, such as vocalization, gestures, or alternative communication systems (picture-based systems, communication technology).

Speech generating devices (SGDs) can be helpful tools in these cases, and there are a variety of communication apps that can be used on handheld electronic devices.

Lani's Story

Lani is the mother of a child with mild autism. Her son is verbal and has no trouble socializing in school or with friends, but still struggles with social cues.

Lani's approach to teaching her son social skills is doing it in a gentle, non-intrusive way. She encourages him to behave according to the situation but she does not force him. She has a set of expectations for polite social norms and where they should be used, and she has explained the reasoning behind them.

Her son shows talent for music and programming and has a very good chance of developing a successful career in either of these fields. Lani knows that he will have to stand up for himself and connect with others, and for this, he will need some level of fluency regarding social norms. She wants her son to be able to be himself but also to have the tools and resources to succeed in life and get along with others.

WHY SOCIAL SKILLS MATTER FOR AUTISTIC CHILDREN

While not everyone, regardless of whether they are autistic or not, needs to excel socially, it's undeniable that social skills play a crucial role in numerous areas of life. For individuals on the autism spectrum, developing and honing these skills can have far-reaching benefits that extend beyond mere social interaction. Let's see some of the ways in which autistic individuals can benefit from the acquisition of social skills:

- **Language development:** Children start developing their language skills within the context of social interactions. Through conversations, interactions, and shared experiences with others, children learn to associate words with objects and events, understand abstract language, and grasp the subtleties of communication. By engaging in meaningful social interactions, autistic individuals can enhance their language skills, facilitating both expressive and receptive communication abilities.
- **Classroom performance:** Social skills such as active listening, asking questions, and participating in group activities are integral to academic success. In the classroom setting, effective communication and collaboration with peers and teachers are essential for understanding and retaining information, engaging in meaningful discussions, and completing tasks successfully. By honing their social skills, autistic individuals can improve their classroom performance and maximize their academic potential.

- **Behavior:** Social acceptance by peers, access to social support networks, and effective emotional management skills are closely linked to behavioral regulation and self-control in youth. Research has shown that a sense of belonging and acceptance within social groups can mitigate behavioral problems and promote positive adjustment in autistic individuals. By fostering meaningful peer relationships and developing effective coping strategies for managing emotions, autistic children can reduce the incidences of disruptive behaviors and enhance their overall well-being.

- **Self-esteem:** Successful peer relationships and a sense of belonging within social groups are critical factors in building self-esteem and self-confidence. For autistic individuals who may face challenges in social interaction, the development of meaningful connections with peers can provide validation, support, and a sense of identity. By experiencing acceptance and inclusion within social settings, autistic individuals can bolster their self-esteem and resilience, reducing the risk of depression, anxiety, and low self-worth.

- **Adaptive functioning:** Social skills serve as the foundation for adaptive functioning in various life aspects, including independent living and employment. In order to navigate the complexities of everyday life and interact effectively with others, individuals on the spectrum must possess a repertoire of social skills that enable them to communicate, collaborate, and problem-solve in diverse social contexts. By acquiring and refining these skills, autistic individuals can enhance their adaptive functioning and achieve greater independence and autonomy in their personal and professional lives.

Mr. Barrett and Ms. Smith's Story

Mr. Barrett and Ms. Smith are special educators in a public school. They have agreed to be part of a study about the benefits of learning outdoors for autistic students. Their goal is to help their students develop some social skills, such as how to appropriately engage in conversation, verbally express their feelings, recognize other people's feelings, problem-solve, deal with frustration, and complete tasks that they find boring.

The classes were held in several outdoor locations of the school, including a blacktop area where the children could draw with chalk, the picnic area, the park, the playground, and the pavilion. The children were allowed to play in the park during class breaks, and the teachers utilized several games and experiments to talk about emotions and emotional regulation. Although the students worked in groups, they were encouraged to make individual choices if they wanted to.

Despite some challenges, like the weather or occasional distractions, the teachers found that their students were more focused and listened better while outdoors. Students prone to shouting or interrupting were also calmer. As they had more space and permission to move and fidget, they had an easier time regulating their emotions.

DEVELOPING SOCIAL SKILLS

Social skills for children include:

- conversation skills, like choosing what to talk about or what body language to use
- play skills, like taking turns in games or sharing toys
- emotional skills, like managing emotions and understanding how others feel
- problem-solving skills, like dealing with conflict or making decisions in social situations

Social skills can be learned and bettered with practice. There are several strategies that can help your child with building their social skills:

- **Practice play:** You can practice play or use stuffed animals to act out social situations, play movement games, board games, or any games that involve multiple people or taking turns.
- **Praise:** It is important to praise and encourage your child when they positively interact with others.
- **Social skills training:** This kind of training is a more structured way of developing social skills.
- **Role-play:** Role-play can be helpful before events, play dates, or any situation that requires socializing. For older children, you can set up situations that involve a social problem and role-play possible solutions and answers.

- **Visual supports:** Pictures, cards, words, and checklists are a good way of learning new skills and refreshing skills already known.
- **Social stories:** Social stories explain social situations in a simple way and discuss the behaviors associated with them.
- **Video-modeling:** Through a video representation of a skill or behavior your child can learn these skills, copy them, and revisit them if necessary.

Socializing is a big part of human life, and most of it is usually learned through experience and contact with others. Autistic people specifically struggle with socialization due to developmental issues, but this doesn't mean that they can't achieve these skills through other means. Helping them develop social skills is a key element of fostering their independence, helping them advocate for their needs and wants, and preparing them for adulthood.

CHAPTER 8
SELF-ADVOCACY, INDEPENDENCE, AND TRANSITIONING TO ADULTHOOD

Stephen Shore's Story

S tephen was diagnosed with autism at a young age, at a time when ASD as a condition was not as researched. When he was two years old, he started losing his language skills. Instead of seeing his diagnosis as a setback, his parents decided to encourage his particular strengths and potential, fostering a home environment where his abilities were celebrated. At age four, Stephen had regained his language skills and started showing a special interest in music.

Stephen's parents emphasized the importance of embracing diversity and accepting differences. They instilled in him a sense of self-worth and confidence, which in turn empowered him to pursue his passions and excel academically and in other aspects of his life. He went to college to become a special education professor, and later, he attended Yale University, where he earned a doctorate in Special Education.

Supported by the love, encouragement, and faith of his family, Stephen went on to become a speaker, author, and advocate for autistic individuals and a living testament of the power of parental and familial acceptance, empathy, and support in the lives of autistic people.

TEACHING YOUR CHILD SELF-ADVOCACY

As a parent, one of the best things you can do is teach your children to advocate for themselves. This becomes twice as important if your child is autistic, as they will have a special set of needs and preferences that not everyone will understand or take into consideration.

Jay's Story

Jay is an autistic child with a severe peanut allergy. When he was in preschool, he had a severe reaction to a cookie that contained peanuts, which put him in the hospital. This experience impacted Jay deeply, and he learned to be extremely careful with his food.

Encouraged by his parents, Jay learned to always check his food for peanut traces and to ask adults around him to help him. If he's not sure, he would rather not eat it to avoid any possible reactions.

How to Teach Self-Advocacy

- **Teach communications skills:** Communication is the base of self-advocacy. You should encourage your child to be vocal about their needs and wants.

If your child has communication issues, you can consider speech therapy or an alternate system of communication.

- **Help your child be comfortable making decisions:** Giving your child choices is a good way of getting them used to making decisions. You can start with simple choices like choosing between two snacks and work your way up to more important subjects. It is also important to make your children understand that decisions have consequences and that, as grown-ups, their choices will be their own.

- **Encourage them to speak up about their needs and preferences:** In order for your child to express what they want or need, you have to let them know that it's ok to do so. They can practice expressing their preferences to you and then try doing it at school, at the doctor's office, and so on.

- **Let your child struggle to solve the problem:** As a parent, your first instinct when you see your child struggling with a problem will be to help them. Though it is difficult to hold back, your child will benefit from trying to come up with a solution on their own. You can always monitor them and be ready to assist them if the situation proves to be beyond their skills.

- **Teach them to negotiate:** Negotiation is a part of our everyday life in one way or another and is a valuable life skill that your child should learn.

- **Help your child better understand others' perspectives:** A big part of self-advocacy is understanding that other people might differ about certain topics. It is important to teach your child to consider those differences.

DEVELOPING INDEPENDENCE

Encouraging your child to be independent is as important as self-advocacy is in their journey to adulthood. Independence skills can be practiced from a young age and can ease the transitional period to adulthood.

These are some things you can do to foster your child's independence:

- **Strengthen communication:** As we've seen, communication goes beyond the spoken language. If your child is fully or partially verbal, you can encourage them to practice their verbal communication or consider if speech therapy is needed. You can introduce them to alternative forms of communication if they are non-verbal or if they prefer to communicate in other ways sometimes. No matter the way, strengthening your child's communication skills will help them to be more independent.
- **Introduce a visual schedule:** Visual schedules can help your child transition between activities without needing an explicit indication. Review the schedule with them beforehand and remind them to check it. Eventually, they will need less and less support, and they will be able to complete their tasks in a more independent way.

- **Work on self-care skills:** The younger your child is, the easier it will be to learn self-care skills such as brushing their teeth or combing their hair. Making these activities a part of their routine will ensure that they get used to them.

- **Teach your child to ask for a break:** It is important that your child has the means of asking for a break when they need it by asking verbally, using a card, or having a "break" button in their communication device. Knowing they can ask for a break at any time will help your child to be more in control of their environment.

- **Work on household chores:** Giving your child a household chore that they can manage will teach them responsibility and involve them in the family routine. If your child struggles with understanding the chore, you can divide it into small steps and model the chore to make it easier for them.

- **Practice money skills:** Knowing how to use money is a valuable life skill. You can introduce your child to it by making them hand the money over for groceries at the store or encouraging them to pay for their snacks.

- **Teach community safety skills:** Teach your children pedestrian safety, how to identify signs and safety markers, how to properly use public transportation, and other travel safety rules that you consider convenient. If needed, you can provide your child with an ID card with their name, diagnosis, and an emergency contact.

- **Build leisure skills:** Encourage your child to do independent hobbies and activities that cater to their interests.
- **Teach self-care during adolescence:** When your child becomes a teenager, you can add to the self-care skills they have learned as a child. You can provide visual aids or a step list for their hygiene routine, make them a checklist, and put together a hygiene kit for them. Make sure to give them encouragement and positive feedback as they learn to master their routine.
- **Work on vocational skills:** Help your child make a list of their strengths, skills, and interests, and look for activities related to their vocational objectives. Consider your child's life skills and start planning for the transition into adulthood.

TRANSITIONING INTO ADULTHOOD

Most people start transitioning into adulthood as they leave high school, start college, or get a job. But for teenagers with ASD and their families, this change is bigger as they enter the adult disability system.

What Do We Mean by "Transition?"

Autistic people who are part of the U.S. special education system start "transitioning" into adulthood when they are 16 years old. Around that age, the school system starts helping them plan their adult life and consider their options, be it college, vocational schools, or employment programs.

The adult disability system is very different from its children's counterparts. While students who qualify for disability services are guaranteed support until they leave high school or turn 21, the adult system is centered around funding and availability. A person might qualify for support, but this support is not always guaranteed.

Youth With Autism at Risk After High School

The transition from high school to college marks a significant milestone for all students, but for autistic individuals, it often comes accompanied with its own adjustments and challenges. Unlike high school, where they were supported by an Individualized Education Plan (IEP) outlining specific accommodations and services, college presents a different landscape. Autistic students no longer have the safety net of an IEP automatically providing accommodations; instead, they must take the initiative to request the accommodations they need, and colleges are required to provide them "within reason."

The shift in responsibility can be daunting for many autistic students, who might feel overwhelmed by the prospect of advocating for themselves in a new and unfamiliar environment. However, those who are accustomed to self-advocacy and have developed effective communication and problem-solving skills are more likely to navigate this system with greater ease. By understanding their rights under the Americans with Disabilities Act (ADA) and proactively engaging with disability support services on campus, autistic students can access the accommodations and resources they need to succeed academically and socially.

The world after high school can be difficult for those on the spectrum, as they might struggle with jobs, education, and navigating society as adults. This doesn't mean, however, that this transition can't be eased. Parents and caregivers play a crucial role in providing emotional support, guidance, and being advocates during this transition process. Similarly, educators and other school staff can provide valuable assistance and resources to help autistic students navigate the college environment.

Start Transition Planning Early

It's never too early to start making plans for your child's future. While you might not know their skills or interests when they are very young, you can start teaching them everyday life skills that will transition into adulthood, like personal hygiene, household chores, or money handling.

A Focus on Daily Living Skills in the Transition Years

School IEPs do not always consider daily living skills (i.e., travel training), but you can request them to be added to your child's plan, as children with ASD are more likely to struggle with these types of skills, no matter their intellectual development.

When considering career paths or potential jobs with your child, take their skills and interests into account, as an obsession with certain topics can be turned into a career if properly directed.

My daughter Lizzie has a hard time understanding how commerce works, and she doesn't understand the value of things. When she was about 16, she had a little money from her birthday or Christmas, and she wanted to use it while we were out shopping. Her mom and I didn't know how much, or in this case, little, she had, and I wish we'd checked before going into the store.

Her brother and sister were able to pick out a couple of things with their money, so we assumed Lizzie had $20 or $30 to spend. We were wrong. When she got up to the counter, the cashier rang up all the toys, and it came to $30 or so. Lizzie pulled out $5 and expected to be able to buy all these toys.

Her mom struggled to make Lizzie understand not only did she not have enough for these things, but this store wouldn't have anything for that amount. She started to have a meltdown at the cash register because she didn't understand why she couldn't buy anything. She had "money." The issue, of course, was that she didn't have enough money. She had a meltdown for five minutes or so at the register before her mom was able to get her out of the store, and she continued to melt down outside. We let her find her calm, but she continued to want to spend her money on something that day and continued to ask us at every stop we made. We eventually allowed her to buy a piece of candy before going home.

Having these situations happen in public can be embarrassing, especially when your child is a teenager or adult. There have been times I wished I was wearing a shirt that announced my daughter has autism. Mental health issues are things we can't see, and society expects people to act a certain way. You begin to feel like a failure as a parent when these happen in public for the world to see. Put it in the back of your mind. You're not a failure; you're helping your child find their place in an overstimulated world.

Transitioning into adulthood is a complicated moment for every teenager, but even more for those who, like autistic teenagers, have challenges of their own related to a condition. In order to ensure that your child will have the smoothest transition possible and the best adult life that they can have, it is important that you give them the tools and skills that will allow them to advocate for their needs, live as independently as possible, and pursue the jobs or careers most suited to them.

CHAPTER 9
NAVIGATING THE HEALTHCARE SYSTEM

Healthcare in the U.S. is set up to accommodate people with different disabilities or disadvantages. Sadly, autism is not one of them. This has resulted in autistic people not receiving adequate care, having mental and physical conditions dismissed and left untreated, more extensive treatments or surgeries, and possibly life-threatening conditions ignored by healthcare professionals.

HEALTHCARE BARRIERS

Autistic people encounter many barriers related to their condition. While access to healthcare should not be a barrier, it is a big concern for those on the spectrum due to several reasons:

Communication

Communication barriers pose significant challenges for individuals with ASD, particularly in the context of medical care. Autism spectrum disorder encompasses a wide range of communication abilities, from completely verbal individuals to those who are non-verbal or rely on alternative communication devices. This can make assessing a patient very complicated, on top of the anxiety and pain the person might be feeling.

Healthcare providers and their ability to communicate with the patient can represent a barrier of their own. While communication in autism varies, being non-verbal does not mean being unable to understand. Individuals with ASD are often highly capable of comprehension and may experience frustration when their communication needs are not met. The healthcare system provides communication services for people who are deaf, blind, or who speak a different language, but has failed to incorporate people with ASD into those in need of assistance.

Healthcare providers must recognize and accommodate the diverse communication needs of individuals with ASD. Understanding and adapting to these differences is essential for providing quality care and ensuring that patients feel understood and supported throughout their medical experience.

Environment and Sensory Needs

The healthcare environment is fast-paced, noisy, filled with strange smells, and usually very bright. It can be stressful and anxiety-producing for someone sensitive and already distressed by an illness.

The environment has a deep impact on autistic people, but providers tend to overlook the sensory issues of the condition. Overexposure to this environment, on top of an illness or pain, can lead to challenging behaviors, aggression, or even injuries.

Lack of Knowledge of Healthcare Providers and Staff

It is important to remember that, outside of autism specialized centers and doctor's offices, healthcare providers are not familiar with autistic special needs. Despite the exponential increase in autism diagnoses over the past few decades, medical curricula have been slow to adapt to the evolving landscape of autism care.

As a result, healthcare providers often lack the specialized knowledge and practical skills to recognize and address the unique needs of individuals with autism. This gap in knowledge can be detrimental for those on the spectrum seeking medical care, as it can lead medical providers to misinterpret behaviors associated with autism, leading to misdiagnosis or inappropriate treatment.

STRATEGIES TO OVERCOME BARRIERS

Navigating the complexities of the healthcare system can be daunting for autistic people, their families, and caregivers, but there are some steps that can be taken to overcome these challenges and ensure a successful consultation.

First Things First

Communication lies at the heart of every successful doctor interaction, so you need to establish a form of communication at the beginning of the medical consult. Healthcare systems are very fast-paced, which causes doctors and other providers to talk quickly and use many medical terms. You need to let them know of the particular needs of your child (such as preferences for verbal or non-verbal communication, use of visual supports, or reliance on alternative communication devices) so they can adopt an adequate pace and explain themselves with a vocabulary everyone can understand.

Preparation for a Non-emergent Visit

Preparing your child for a visit to the hospital or the doctor's office is the most important part and can also significantly impact their experience and outcome, particularly in emergent situations.

You can use a social story, a video, or cue cards to explain what the visit will entail and what behavior is expected of them. These visual tools can help provide a clear and concrete explanation of what to expect during the visit, including procedures, the role of healthcare providers, and the behavior expected of them. By familiarizing your child with the sights, sounds, and routines of the hospital or doctor's office beforehand, you can help reduce uncertainty and fear, empowering them to feel more in control of the situation.

In the case of emergent visits, you should advocate for your child as if their life depended on it. This may involve clearly communicating your child's medical history, symptoms, and any relevant information to healthcare providers, as well as advocating for their needs and preferences throughout the treatment process.

Advocate, Advocate, and Advocate Some More

Educate yourself on disability laws and be aware of what your child's rights are when it comes to healthcare.

Request a quieter or even a private area for your child to be in, and don't be afraid of making reasonable adjustments to control the sensory environment (i.e., dimming the lights and turning off the TV)

Avoid having multiple persons talking or examining your child at the same time, unless it is absolutely necessary, to avoid overwhelming them. Be aware that this could happen if you are in a teaching hospital, so communicate your child's needs to their doctors and nurses.

If it's a non-emergency visit or a hospital stay, bring comfort objects from home and any sensory aid that they might need.

HOW TO ADVOCATE FOR YOUR CHILD IN A MEDICAL SETTING

Merriam-Webster defines advocacy as "the act or process of supporting a cause or proposal." (Merriam-Webster, 2019). Autistic children will need multiple health-related consults and services throughout their childhoods and even as adults, so advocacy is crucial to help them navigate the fast-paced healthcare system and its changes.

Things to Know Before You Get Started on Your Advocacy Journey

- **Physician knowledge:** It is important to understand that not all healthcare providers will be aware of your child's needs or will have the knowledge or training for it. Sadly, research has shown that medical students don't receive sufficient training in treating autistic children and aren't able to manage care for them.

- **Family knowledge:** The role of parents and caregivers as advocates of an autistic child is an ongoing process throughout their childhood. In order to properly advocate for your child, you will need to educate yourself on the other medical areas related to ASD and its co-morbid conditions. Being aware of the care and services your child needs can be overwhelming, but knowing why they need them will make the task less intimidating.

- **Language:** If English is not your first language, you might find that the language barrier can make your navigation through the healthcare system difficult. You can look for organizations that provide support to non-English speaking families and check your healthcare supportive services before any appointment.

- **Stigma:** Social stigma and ignorance around autism can contribute to autistic people and their families feeling isolated and avoiding engaging with the healthcare system.

How to Advocate for Your Child

- **Awareness:** It is critical that you are aware of your child's particular diagnosis, their risks for other conditions, and their need for support. You are the person who knows them best. Being aware of their needs will allow you to be their voice. Know the choices available if you are not satisfied with the medical care received or with the professionals, and don't stay with a provider who lacks the knowledge or the will to provide your child with the best care possible.

- **Prepare your child and your provider for visits:** In the same way you prepare your child for a visit to the doctor with stories and other tools, you can communicate with your provider to discuss your child's needs. If they are better prepared, the chances of a successful visit will increase.

- **Collaborate with your child's healthcare provider:** Medical providers are a part of your team. Your collaboration is crucial, especially if your child is unable to self-report symptoms. If you feel your medical providers and staff are not collaborative, you can request a meeting with management to discuss ways to better work together. Work with them and make the suggestions you deem necessary.

- **Understand your child's rights:** The Americans with Disabilities Act (ADA) guarantees equal access to healthcare for disabled people, including those with autism. Familiarizing yourself with the law will help you know how it applies to your child and how to request accommodations for equal access.

The reality of the healthcare system will sadly mean that you and your child will encounter barriers in your search for proper attention and support. Do not let this reality discourage you. In order to be a better advocate for your child's needs, familiarize yourself with the medical and legal knowledge related to autism and promote better communication with your providers so you all can work together in doing what's best for your child.

CHAPTER 10

NAVIGATING THE EDUCATION SYSTEM

A s a parent, you are the best advocate for your child when it comes to working with the school district. A well-written Individualized Education Plan (IEP) is essential in planning your child's education and setting the goals for their future.

An IEP should be construed in collaboration with parents, teachers, and therapists and should detail the strategies, needs, services, and supports necessary for the child's success.

CHOOSING THE RIGHT PROGRAM FOR YOUR CHILD

Irene's Story

Irene has an autistic son and has been looking for a suitable school for him. She visited several specialized autistic schools, but she found that the teachers and directors usually lacked the proper knowledge about the condition and that some of these schools were more interested in containing the children instead of helping them develop their skills.

Having turned to traditional private schooling, Irene found that most of them were focused mainly on achievement and excellence. The teachers didn't really care about children who were different and who needed particular guidance and care.

Lastly, she decided to try her luck with public schooling in her area. She asked if they would accept her child along with a therapeutic companion, but she was denied, as the school authorities considered that the rest of the students and their parents were not prepared to deal with the reality of autism.

Every autistic child has their own needs and requirements, which means that not all schooling programs will be suitable for them. When choosing your child's school you need to consider the differences between programs and the particular needs of your child.

When considering schools, take into account your child's skill set, intellectual development, support needs, therapy requirements, and physical limitations. You will also need to consider your needs as a parent and what you require in terms of communication and assistance when researching possible schools.

Public School

Public School Classrooms

Autistic children didn't always attend public schooling, as they were collectively regarded as non-verbal, of uncertain behavior, and difficult to manage. This view has changed, and due to this, educators have improved their knowledge about autism, and there are more services available for children with ASD.

Not all autistic children present intellectual delays, and many of them are able to attend traditional public schooling, with or without an IEP or 504 plan. In this context, they will be able to socially interact with different kinds of students.

Public School With Resource Room Support

If your child requires specialized instruction to meet their behavioral, social, and intellectual needs but you still want them to attend public school, they might require additional support.

Special education teachers can work with your child in or out of the regular education classroom and assist them with regulating their behavior, interacting with their peers, their speech, and their classes.

Public Schools With Functional Support

Some autistic children with health-related needs, behavioral issues, intellectual delays, or speech impediments might require a functional classroom while attending public schooling. Depending on their skill levels, they might require these services all day or during a part of the day.

Children who require functional classrooms due to their feeding skills, their need for assistance going to the bathroom, or their communication skills might still be able to and enjoy attending some regular classes and interacting with their peers during recess or in non-classroom settings.

Public Schools With ABA Services

Some children might qualify for Applied Behavior Analysis (ABA) services. In these cases, a board-certified analyst can come to school and assist teachers with working with children on the spectrum.

Private School

For some autistic children, private school might be the better option due to a multitude of reasons. However, it is important to remember that private schools are not under the mandate to provide specialized instruction and services as public schools are.

If you prefer your child to attend private schooling, you need to disclose their diagnosis to the staff and inform them of your child's unique needs and requirements, their sensitivities, the tools that they will need, and how to properly manage their mood.

Private School for Children With Autism

A private school that specializes in autism is also an option. These schools deal specifically with students on the spectrum, and their staff has received specific training to deal with the academic, behavioral, and social needs of autistic students. A possible drawback, though, of this kind of schooling is the lack of interaction with non-autistic peers.

Homeschooling

Some parents might prefer educating their autistic children at home due to personal or religious reasons or due to a dissatisfaction with the public system. Homeschooling has the advantage of allowing the parents direct and daily input into their child's education, but you need to consider alternate ways to provide your child opportunities to practice and develop their social skills, especially if they are homeschooled on their own.

Combining Home and Public Schooling

If you decide to homeschool your child, you might find that there are some skills that you are unable or unwilling to help with. You can inquire with your public school about the possibility of your child attending certain classes during a portion of the day in order for them to develop a particular skill.

BENEFITS OF ADVOCATING FOR YOUR CHILD AT SCHOOL

There will never be a disadvantage to being an advocate for your child, but by advocating for them in the school setting, you will get specific benefits:

- It helps you obtain an Individualized Education Plan (IEP) that considers your child's specific needs, goals, and strengths and ensures that they will receive the necessary educational support and accommodation.

- It helps to fix potential issues that might arise in the school.
- It helps your child develop self-advocacy.
- It keeps you informed about your child's progress.
- It helps to achieve inclusion for your child and, by setting precedents and demanding equality, also achieves inclusion for other special needs students who are not receiving equal opportunities.

HOW TO ADVOCATE FOR YOUR CHILD IN SCHOOL

- **Be well-informed about your child's needs:** In order to know what services and practices are the most suited to your child, you need to be informed about their particular diagnosis and the possible treatments. Learn about the rights and services available under the current laws about education and disabilities.
- **Be prepared:** The public school system usually offers state-funded training for parents. Conferences and other types of training are also available and are a good resource to learn about the school system, federal and state laws, and autism treatments. Local parent groups can offer support and information.
- **Remain focused on the child:** Meetings and IEP planning can be complicated if parents and teachers have contradicting opinions and strategies.

Remember that collaboration fosters progress and that all of you have the common goal of doing what's best for your child.

- **Communicate clearly:** Communication is key to being a successful advocate. Communicating with teachers and other school staff can be made difficult by the use of educational jargon, acronyms, and specialized terms. On the other hand, parent communication will naturally have an emotional component to it, and it might be influenced by past mistakes or concerns. Remember that the clearer the communication, the better you will be able to collaborate.

- **Be proactive, not reactive:** Prepare for meetings in advance and have a list of topics to cover. If you feel that a meeting is turning negative or confrontational, take a break or end the meeting early to avoid worsening the situation.

- **Ask questions:** Be sure to ask for clarification of the terms, procedures, and regulations you don't understand or find confusing. Understanding the planning and getting answers can help reduce your frustration and ease any concerns you might have about your child's schooling. Be assertive in your communication with the school and collaborate to create an open and trusting relationship.

- **Know your rights:** Be aware of alternate possibilities and legal rights in advance so you can focus on the meetings and properly advocate for your child's wellbeing.

- **Inclusion:** The inclusion of autistic children into a regular classroom presents many benefits and is more related to the school's attitude than to a certain program. It will give you and your child a sense of belonging and community and facilitate social interaction and skill development. Remember that your child has a right to inclusion.

UNDERSTANDING EDUCATIONAL RIGHTS AND LAWS

A Child's Rights for Public Education

Special needs children's right to education is protected under the Individuals with Disabilities Education Act (IDEA), which ensures that each state provides all children with a public education according to their particular needs. In addition, children with disabilities are entitled to early intervention services and special education.

This legislation also protects the parents' and caregivers' right to be treated as equals by the different school districts and gives them the right to decide on their children's education plans. This not only allows you as a parent to advocate for your child but also ensures that you will be an active and informed participant in the planning and monitoring of your child's educational plan.

What is a "Free and Appropriate Public Education" (FAPE)?

This legislation guarantees "free and appropriate public education" for all children with disabilities. It is important to highlight the use of the word "appropriate," as it relates to the particular needs of every child. An appropriate education is one with a plan tailored to every specific individual.

But even if you and your children's therapists want to provide your child with the best program possible, school districts are required to only provide an appropriate one. It is necessary, then, to work collaboratively with the school and your providers to negotiate the best plan possible within the school's capabilities.

What is the "Least Restrictive Environment" (LRE)?

IDEA also states that your child should be placed in the "least restricted environment," meaning an environment where they are able to interact with abled children in a regular class setting. This ensures that your child, according to their abilities and needs, will be included in a general education setting.

While in some cases, autistic children might thrive in a regular classroom on their own or with special support, you should consider if this inclusion is the right decision for your child, who might need a special education program, a specialized school, or homeschooling.

Early Intervention Services (EI)

The Individuals with Disabilities Education Act also provides funds to create early intervention programs at no cost for children under three with developmental delays or conditions that might result in a developmental delay.

These services vary from state to state, but they all should be tailored to the child's unique needs. After a comprehensive evaluation, EI services should provide an Individual Family Service Plan (IFSP) where the child's current levels of development and functioning and the provided goals are described.

The goal of EI services is to minimize the impact of the disability on the child's development and they include, among others, speech and language instruction, occupational therapy, applied behavior analysis, and psychological evaluation. They might also include family training and counseling.

Special Education Services

Special education services pick up from where EI services leave off after the child turns three. These services are provided through the public school system, and their focus differs from that of early intervention.

Where IE services attend to the child's overall development, special education services are focused on the child's education, no matter their current level of disability. They are in charge of collaborating with parents and caregivers in developing an Individualized Education Plan (IEP) that describes your child's unique educational needs and the ways they will be met.

An IEP should describe your child's strengths and weaknesses, a set of goals and objectives to reach, and a detailed program to do so.

Extended School Year (ESY) Services

In those cases where it is proven that a disabled child will experience a regression in skill during school breaks, they might be considered eligible for Extended School Year (ESY) services. These services are provided during long school breaks to prevent substantial regressions, but they will not be geared toward the acquisition of new skills.

Family involvement and communication with the school are crucial in setting the child's objectives and determining the need for these services, as well as providing consistency between the school and home environments.

How to Get Services Started for a Child?

For children under three, you should call your local Early Intervention Agency. For older children, you can contact your school district's Special Education department.

Before providing any services, further assessments and evaluations might be needed, such as a parent interview, a speech-language assessment, an evaluation of current behavior, or a developmental evaluation, among others.

The waiting time required for the completion of the evaluations can be frustrating for parents, but these assessments will provide in-depth information about your child's symptoms, strengths, and needs and will be helpful in the planning of services.

Rights to Assistive Technology

The development of new technologies has created new opportunities for the inclusion of autistic persons in society, and this is also true when it comes to education. The IDEA requires schools to include assistive technology to meet the needs of their students, and as a parent, you have the right to require it as well.

As the school district is responsible for meeting the student's assistive technology needs, lack of funding or teacher training cannot be cited as an excuse for denying assistive technology devices.

If an IEP meeting is unable to determine the best assistive technology services for your child or if you disagree with the school's decision, a formal assistive technology evaluation might be required.

WORKING TOGETHER: TEACHERS AND PARENTS

The success of a child's formal education is built on the collaboration between their family and their teachers. When it comes to children with autism, their unique needs, strengths, and challenges require a close partnership between parents and teachers to provide the best possible support and opportunities for learning and growth.

Begin With Open Communication

Be it formal or informal encounters, consistent communication with your child's teachers is key to ensuring that all parties are updated on the child's progress, any current or new challenges, and any changes in behavior or academic performance.

Share with the teachers any insights about your child's preferences, habits, and triggers. This will help them understand your child better and to adapt their teaching accordingly.

Develop an Individualized Education Plan (IEP)

Being involved in the development of your child's IEP is the best way to ensure that it is tailored to their unique needs. But also keep in mind that children grow and evolve, so it is necessary to reassess the IEP regularly and modify it as needed.

Offer Resources and Training

Not all teachers are trained in autism or have experience with autistic students. You can help them by sharing resources, articles, and books that have helped you in understanding your child's needs and learning preferences. You can also encourage your school and your school district to offer specialized training opportunities that can help equip teachers with the knowledge and skills needed to effectively support autistic students in the classroom.

Foster a Consistent Environment

Collaboration between home and school is essential for promoting consistency and continuity in your child's learning environment. Work with your teachers to establish consistent routines, expectations, and strategies that can be implemented both at home and in the classroom.

Sharing successful strategies and techniques that have worked with your child at home can help their teachers create a supportive and familiar environment that facilitates learning and development.

Encourage Social Interaction

Collaboration between parents and teachers can also play an important role in promoting social interaction and skill development. By working together to develop social stories, plan interactions with peers, and organize group activities or playdates, parents and teachers can create opportunities for meaningful social engagement and growth.

Advocate for Your Child

While it is important to trust your child's teachers, advocating for your child's needs is equally crucial. Don't hesitate to speak up and request additional support, accommodations, or modifications to the classroom environment if necessary. Your advocacy assures that your child's needs are recognized and addressed, which will ultimately support their success and well-being in school.

Celebrate Progress, Not Just Achievements

Celebrate your child's everyday victories, no matter how small, and be patient. Progress can be gradual, but by acknowledging and celebrating each step forward, you will reinforce your child's confidence and motivation to continue learning and growing.

Navigating the educational system as a parent of an autistic child can be difficult due to the variety of options, plans, and teaching methods. But remember that there will be an option that is best suited to your child and their needs, and that is your child's right to receive an education that will help them develop their skills in the best way possible.

CHAPTER 11

PLANNING FOR THE FUTURE

C hange is always difficult for an autistic child, no matter how small the change might seem. A major change, like a parent or caregiver passing away, can turn their world upside down. Therefore, it is crucial that you plan the care and support your child might need in the event of your death.

LEGAL PLANNING

If your child's disability will require life-long assistance, legal planning is essential. There are several ways to provide them with legal support in the least restrictive manner possible, but these will vary according to your state's laws. It is important, then, to seek legal counsel who is familiar with your state's legislation.

Supported Decision-Making (SDM)

Supported decision-making is a way for people with disabilities to receive help with important decisions without giving up their legal rights. It's an alternative to other forms like conservatorships, guardianships, or powers of attorney, but is currently only recognized by a few states.

Many families have informally adopted SDM principles with their children, creating a network of trusted people around them who can advise, give options, and help make informed decisions. This support can be related to healthcare, finances, living arrangements, relationships, employment, and many other situations.

This form of support allows the individual to express their goals and preferences and reach them with the help of their support network.

Conservatorship and Guardianship

Conservatorship and guardianship are often used interchangeably. They don't have a standardized legal definition and they vary from state to state. Guardianship is typically used in relation to minors, while a Conservatorship usually applies to 18 and older individuals. The scope of decisions affected by these forms will also vary according to state laws.

Both are legal arrangements where a court-appointed individual is given the authority to make personal decisions on behalf of someone unable to make decisions by themselves. These arrangements can be related to financial decisions, healthcare, and well-being, or they can give authority for broader decision-making.

The court-appointed conservator or guardian will be decided by a judge and might be a parent, a family member, a friend, or a neutral party. While you, as a parent, can propose a guardian or conservator, the court is not required to oblige, and the decision will be up to the judge. Conservators and guardians are responsible for acting in the best interest of their ward, and they should honor their right to decide about matters not affected by the guardianship or conservatorship.

It is important to remember that an individual under a conservatorship or a guardianship is unable to do anything considered a "legal contract," which includes opening bank accounts, taking out loans, getting married, signing business contracts, buying or selling property, or, in some states, voting. You should always consult your lawyer about the specific rights that will be retained and limited according to your state's legislation.

Power of Attorney (POA)

Power of attorney is a legal document where an individual, who is considered capable of making decisions, gives someone else the authority to make decisions on their behalf. This form can vary according to the type of decision and the circumstances:

- **General POA:** Gives broad decision-making authority.
- **Limited POA:** Gives authority over specific matters.
- **Durable POA:** Remains in effect even if the person becomes incapable of making decisions.

- **Springing POA:** Becomes effective when a specific event or condition occurs.
- **Healthcare POA:** Gives authority over matters related to healthcare.
- **Financial POA:** Gives authority over matters related to finances.

A power of attorney does not override the individual's capacity to make decisions or their ability to enter legal contracts. It is a helpful tool for caregivers to access medical records, communicate with medical providers, pay bills, fill out taxes, and sign paperwork. In the event of a court-appointed conservatorship or guardianship, any power of attorney will be overridden.

When to Start the Process

Planning for your child's future involves more than just educational and medical considerations. There is no set time to start making legal provisions, but it is important to consider these matters before your child reaches adulthood. Some paperwork filing will depend on your child's age and whether they are considered a legal adult.

Legal arrangements can be a complex process, so give yourself ample time to discuss options, gather paperwork, and receive legal advice about your state's specific legislation on these matters.

Personal Rights and Supporting Independence

Supported decision-making, conservatorships, guardianships, and powers of attorney share the goal of helping individuals who might need assistance or are unable to make informed decisions. They are designed to be as least restrictive as possible, and they don't necessarily take away the individual's rights. They might give partial or full authority to the appointed person, but in every case, the disabled person will retain their right to be treated with respect and dignity and to be appropriately taken care of.

These legal forms are intended to be used as a last resort and can be changed according to the needs of the person. It is important that you, as a parent, listen to your child and respect their wants, opinions, and preferences as much as possible.

SPECIAL NEEDS TRUSTS

A special needs trust (SNT) is an arrangement set up for the benefit of a disabled person in order to help them prepare for current or future expenses. It can be used to set aside money, property, or life insurance benefits. The person will benefit from the assets in the trust but they won't own them, which in turn will not impact their eligibility for government benefits such as Medicaid or Supplementary Social Security.

It is important to note that even though many SNTs are created by parents or caregivers, they can also be created by the disabled person in order to protect their assets and avoid losing government benefits.

The Primary Objectives of a Special Needs Trust

The main objective of a special needs trust is to protect the assets left to the disabled beneficiary and to generate additional income to provide them with a better quality of life. A trust also ensures that they are still eligible for government benefits and that they don't become a financial burden to other family members once the parents or primary caregiver are no longer able to care for them. Federal and state benefits will cover basic expenses and healthcare but not specialized treatments, educational programs, therapy equipment, or house modifications.

Expenses to Plan For

- **Healthcare expenses beyond coverage:** Government benefits will cover certain expenses, but there may be gaps in this coverage, particularly when it comes to specialized treatments and interventions. Other additional expenses can be related to dental work, surgeries, medications, and therapies not covered by insurance. These costs can accumulate quickly and need careful financial planning and budgeting.
- **Educational or recreational enrichment programs:** Access to educational and recreational enrichment programs is essential for the development and well-being of your child, but they can come with associated costs, including tuition fees, materials, and participation fees.
- **Behavioral and psychological counseling:** Counseling is an integral component of autism

intervention and support but is not always fully covered by insurance or benefits, leaving families responsible for the out-of-pocket expenses.

- **Personal caregivers:** Many autistic children require additional support and assistance in their daily activities, personal care, and supervision. Whether you hire a personal caregiver as respite care, someone to assist with household tasks, or for one-on-one support, you might incur additional expenses.

- **Transportation:** Some families will have to consider transportation to access medical appointments, therapy sessions, or educational programs, which will come with fuel expenses, public transportation fares, or specialized transportation services.

- **Hobbies and entertainment:** Providing your child with the opportunities to pursue their interests, hobbies, and other recreational activities is an integral part of their development, but it can come with associated costs in equipment, materials, membership fees, or admission fees.

- **Any physical therapy not covered by insurance or benefits:** Insurance and benefits should cover the basic therapy services required by your child, but they won't always cover additional or specialized therapy.

What You Need to Get Started

- Consult an experienced lawyer who can advise you on the matter and prepare the legal paperwork. The requirements for setting up a fund might vary according to state legislation, so it's important to consult an attorney familiar with your state's proceedings and laws.

- Select a trustee who can administer the trust, manage its investments, and monitor the benefits and requests.
- Complete a Letter of Intent. In this document, you can communicate the instructions of the trust regarding the beneficiary's future and you can express how you wish your child to be taken care of.
- Consider the long-term financial needs of your child, their current medical expenses, and any potential change that they might suffer.

Where Do I Get the Money to Fund the Special Needs Trust?

You can fund the trust with assets that you already own, life insurance, or with your estate. In the case of life insurance, the benefit will be directed to the trust in its entirety, and it won't be subjected to taxes. If you decide to leave part of your estate to fund the trust, you will have to name the trust (and not your child) as a beneficiary in your will.

Trust Document Explained

The document will contain a special provision that states that the assets of the trust should be used to supplement your child's benefits and not to replace them. It can also describe how and when the assets can be withdrawn in order to avoid creating family conflicts.

The complexity of the document will vary according to the assets included and should be prepared by an attorney who has experience with special needs documents.

Letter of Intent Explained

The Letter of Intent is not a legal document, but it will help guide the trustee and others involved in the management of the fund. It should describe your child's history, their current needs, and the provisions you want to make for their future. You can modify and adapt its contents as time passes to better reflect your child's needs.

Other Things to Consider

In order for your child to be eligible for government benefits and not lose them later on, they can't own more than a certain amount of assets. You will need to consult with your lawyer or a financial advisor to make sure that any unearned income your child will receive won't jeopardize these benefits. The trust, not your child, should be named as beneficiary on your will, life insurance, retirement funds, and deed.

To ensure that your child will be properly cared for when you are no longer able to be their main caregiver or supporter, you need to make financial and legal provisions for their care. Consult a lawyer and a financial adviser to build a plan that is best suited to your child's needs and requirements.

CHAPTER 12
SELF-CARE FOR PARENTS

THINGS PARENTS SHOULD KNOW

A utism is a developmental disorder. While its causes are not yet fully understood, there is no evidence that it is caused by a parenting style. Instead, it is believed that the condition might be caused by genetics and that certain environmental factors might increase the risk of developing it.

If your child has been diagnosed with ASD, it's not a reflection of you as a parent. You have not failed anything. Being a parent is never easy, even with non-autistic children, and there is no fail-proof manual. It is something that you do with patience and time.

THE CHALLENGES OF PARENTING AUTISTIC CHILDREN

Parents of children with ASD are extraordinary because they need to be. They are parents, a support system, caregivers, enablers of skills and abilities, and much more. Every day presents them with a new challenge and a new opportunity for their children and for themselves. But their child's condition has its own challenges, on top of the usual tests of being a parent:

- **Finances:** Raising a child on the spectrum can come accompanied by long-term financial issues, especially for those families not covered by insurance. Extra medical expenses, transportation, hiring a caregiver, or quitting a job to be more present are all things that can pile up and become a burden. Parents might feel ashamed of asking for help or revealing their situation to friends and family, which can result in additional troubles down the road.

- **Stress:** Being the caregiver of an autistic child is no easy task. Every autistic child is different, and caring for them can be a full-time job. The stress levels are likely to increase, especially for single parents and nuclear families or for those who lack a support network. Daily struggles, additional health issues, and social situations can all have a deep impact on the parent's physical and mental health.

- **No "me" time:** Parents who can't afford to hire help or get it from extended family and friends can struggle with taking care of their child, performing at their job (or jobs), and managing their home and family. Free time for themselves is not a priority, and it's sometimes impossible. With no time to socialize, rest, exercise, or indulge in hobbies and interests, their whole identity is taken over by the responsibility of being a caregiver.

- **Communication with a non-verbal child:** Many autistic children struggle with verbal communication, being unable to communicate their needs and wants, and having difficulty understanding social cues. This can be another challenge for the parents, and it adds to their stress and anxiety.

- **Stigmatization:** Autism is still surrounded by a social stigma as a result of ignorance and disinformation. Not everyone is kind and understanding, and parents of autistic children can encounter negative reactions.

CHANGE YOUR MINDSET

The way in which you approach your particular situation will have an impact on you and your family. Your mindset will be important in taking care of yourself to better the care for your child.

- **Things will be difficult:** There is nothing wrong with accepting that parenting an autistic child is difficult. This doesn't make you a bad parent or diminish your affection for your child.

- **Make a note of the good moments, not just the bad:** Accepting the bad moments does not mean focusing only on them. They will happen, but so will the good moments. Taking time to enjoy the good moments and remembering them will put the hard times into perspective.

- **Ask for help:** You need a little time to yourself to decompress, enjoy a hobby, or just catch up on sleep. Ask the people around you to help with your child for a short time so you can relax and have some "me" time.

- **Don't get caught up with the "super parent" parenting style:** Social media can make us believe that other parents are superheroes who excel at multitasking and never struggle with their children. These posts and accounts are designed to make it look so and give us only a glimpse into their daily lives. Holding yourself up to their standards can lead you to believe that if you are not perfect, you are not good enough, which is simply not true.

- **Stick up for your child without being confrontational:** It can be tempting to raise your voice at ignorant and rude commentators or at teachers and medical providers who can't seem to listen to your concerns, but it isn't worth it. They won't learn or listen better to you. But you can be the better person by educating them or firmly advocating for your child's needs and rights.

- **See a doctor:** Scheduling and attending your own doctor's appointments on top of your child's appointments, therapies, and school meetings is difficult. But you need physical and mental care and support as well, and the stress of being the caregiver of a special needs child can put you at a higher risk for certain conditions.

STRESS MANAGEMENT

It is impossible to avoid stress entirely, no matter how good a mindset and support network you have. Setting up strategies for its management will help you avoid getting overwhelmed during difficult times.

- **Positive thinking and self-talk:** Talking yourself through your feelings and emotions can help you with thinking positively and increase your ability to cope with stressful situations. The more you practice helpful self-talk, the more automatic it will be for you the next time you are feeling overwhelmed.
- **Relaxation and breathing strategies:** The same calming strategies that your child uses to help with emotional regulation can come in handy if you are feeling stressed or overwhelmed. You can also set aside some time to meditate, relax, and practice mindfulness to decompress, be more aware of your thoughts and feelings, and improve your positivity.
- **Get organized:** Feeling that things are out of your control can greatly contribute to stress. Finding ways of getting organized is a way of having more control over things and situations. Make a list of things you need to do and tackle one at a time. You can also implement family routines to get through tasks in a more efficient manner and free up time to enjoy and do fun activities.
- **Find reprieve outside of work:** For many parents, work is one of the places where they have a break from being the main caregiver. This is not ideal and

can interfere with your job. It is important to have a time and space outside of work where you can enjoy yourself, focus on your health, and work on other important relationships.

- **Make time for fun activities for yourself and other family members:** Having a good time can help reduce the whole family's stress levels. It is important that you spend time with your spouse and other children and that you strengthen your relationships with them. Find activities that you enjoy and can do together or own your own.

- **Don't let family traditions and rituals slide:** Family traditions and rituals provide a sense of belonging and unity and help strengthen family relationships, especially during stressful times. Keep in mind that you might have to modify some traditions to suit your autistic child's needs.

- **Ask family and friends to babysit or help out so that you can have a break:** Asking for help can give you time to work on yourself while also allowing your child to spend time and do activities with other family members.

- **Respite care:** Investing in respite care can give you a break without having to resort to friends or extended family. You might be concerned about leaving your child with an outsider, but you can ask for references, conduct an interview, and make time for your child to get to know the respite caregiver before leaving them in their care.

As a parent of a child with ASD, you may feel that your child's needs should always come first, no matter the situation. And while this can be true sometimes, it doesn't mean that you are not entitled to the same physical and mental care that you give to your child. So ask for help, rely on your support network, and take some time off to take better care of yourself and, that way, care better for your child.

CONCLUSION

Autism is a complex condition. Science is still unsure about its causes, and even with all the advances in research and treatments, we are still unable to predict or eradicate it. In addition to this, there are also many issues and comorbidities associated with ASD. The social ignorance and stigma around autism do very little to lighten the burden on autistic people, their families, and caregivers. This can result in unwanted advice, critiques, being ignored or dismissed by medical providers and school staff, or just feeling judged by others for situations that are out of anyone's control.

Contrary to this panorama of uncertainty, we can be sure that autism as a condition is not an obstacle to living a happy and fulfilling life. Throughout the pages of this book, we have tried to dispel myths and beliefs around autism and to give you, as a parent, the tools for a better understanding and support of your child.

We have taken a look into the developmental issues related to autism spectrum disorder and the differences in world-view, sensibilities, and emotions that result from those issues. We have discussed strategies, activities, and resources to overcome challenges like meltdowns and repetitive behaviors, foster their resilience, and improve their emotional well-being.

We have talked about the importance of being an advocate for your child when it comes to healthcare, education, and social situations and the need to help them advocate for themselves. In addition to this, we have discussed the necessity of planning for your child's future as they transition into adults and in the event of you not being their primary caregiver.

Lastly, we have remarked how you, as a parent and caregiver, need to prioritize self-care and your own well-being. Remember that by caring for yourself, you are better equipped to support, care, and advocate for your child.

A central theme of this book is the notion that effective strategies can be powerful tools in helping your child navigate the many challenges they might find in their journey. From therapies to sensory activities to physical tools to the recognition of emotions and feelings on themselves and others, the range of strategies discussed is directed towards the emotional, physical, and mental well-being and the empowerment of your child and of yourself as their parent and supporter.

It is also impossible to overlook the impact that individual stories of resilience can have on us as individuals. As one more of many examples, we have Alex's story:

Alex was a very irritable baby, sensitive to food, water, and noise. When he was around 12 months old, he started losing his speech and his ability to eat solid food. At 18 months old, he was engaging in repetitive behavior, such as clapping and flapping his hands, which resulted in him being diagnosed with ASD.

By age three, Alex had severe developmental delays. He could walk, but not run. He was unable to speak and had extreme sensory issues, which made his daily routine excruciating, as he struggled with being bathed or clothed. He suffered from many comorbidities, had sleeping issues, and was prone to temper tantrums.

His mother was distraught, both from the physical toll of caring for Alex and from the anguish of seeing her son's suffering. Looking for help, she enrolled Alex in an autism treatment program.

Within a short time, Alex started showing signs of improvement. He developed his vocabulary and began asking for things verbally. His sensory issues and repetitive behavior diminished, and a change in his food helped him control some of his digestive problems and allergies. Encouraged by his mother, Alex learned to read and developed a passion for books, which greatly aided his language development.

Motivated by Alex's results, his parents asked their doctor for new evaluations and a program tailored to their child's needs. With this new program's help, Alex was able to crawl, run, climb, and generally move with normality.

Seeing Alex's love for music, his mother taught him the musical notes. Alex proved to have a musical talent, and he was able to teach himself to play songs on a toy piano. He was able to play songs by ear, and he started composing his own little pieces.

By age six, Alex had reached his peers' developmental level intellectually, physically, and socially. He had even surpassed them in some areas. He had an aptitude for languages and computer programming, as well as for piano.

By his ninth birthday, Alex had taken an examination in a conservatory and had done extremely well. He is enrolled in online school and all his teachers describe him as a good student, well-behaved, and very sociable. He loves to ride his bike, play with his friends, and play music. He is thriving academically, socially, and creatively. He has surpassed expectations and embraced life with boundless enthusiasm.

Alex's story is not an isolated triumph but a sign of hope amidst the uncertainties. It underscores the profound impact of early intervention, effective treatments, personalized care, and familial advocacy. His story resonates with countless families navigating the complexities of autism, offering solace, inspiration, and a glimpse of what is possible.

As you reflect on the topics and strategies we have discussed, I encourage you to take on the journey ahead of you with new strength and understanding. Armed with knowledge, compassion, empathy, and love for your child, you possess the ability to shape a life filled with joy, resilience, and growth.

Closing this page, I want to thank you for letting me be a part of your journey. As someone who is also a parent of an autistic child and has gone through the same challenges that you are facing, I know the feelings, questions, and uncertainties that you are facing. I also know that, even when you are feeling frustrated and overwhelmed, there is hope ahead. Your dedication, love, and commitment to your child are the foundation of this journey of parenting.

With each step of this journey, remember that you are not alone: There is a community of fellow parents, professionals, educators, friends, and family that stand ready to help you and walk with you.

GLOSSARY

ABA (Applied Behavior Analysis): The behavioral therapy approach is widely used in autism intervention. It is used to teach basic and social skills in a systematic manner to create a change in behavior, usually on a one-to-one basis.

Advocate: A person who speaks on behalf of another.

Assistive Technology: Technology devices and programs used to assist autistic individuals with communication, education, and daily routines.

Behavioral Therapy: Therapies that attempt to identify and change habits or behavior that is unwanted.

(Autistic) Burnout: State of physical, mental, and emotional exhaustion, diminished capacity for managing life skills, and stress, often caused by sustained overwhelm.

Comorbidity: Also called co-occurring condition, it is any additional medical or psychiatric condition that may occur alongside autism, such as ADHD, anxiety disorders, or intestinal issues.

Developmental Delay: Failure to obtain a developmental milestone in comparison to peers of the same age.

Diagnostic and Statistical Manual (DSM-5): The official system for the classification of psychological and psychiatric disorders prepared and published by the American Psychiatric Association.

Early Intervention: Services, therapy, and medical interventions focused on helping with the developmental delays of children under the age of three.

Echolalia: Repetitive speech or mimicking of words or phrases.

Emotional Regulation: Capacity to emotionally respond to experiences in an appropriate manner.

Executive Functioning: Cognitive processes for planning, organizing, and completing tasks.

Extended School Year Services (ESY): Services provided during extended school breaks to avoid regressions in already learned skills.

Hyperfocus: Intense concentration on a specific interest or activity.

Hypersensitivity: When a person is highly sensitive and may have unusual or extreme reactions to touch, taste, smell, or sounds. It is commonly linked to anxiety and stress.

Hyposensitivity: When a person is under-sensitive or underwhelmed by touch, taste, smell and sound and are likely to seek out additional sensory activity.

IEP (Individualized Education Plan): Tailored educational plan for students with special needs.

Inclusion: Integrating individuals with autism into mainstream activities.

Meltdown: Emotional response usually caused by sensory overload (not to be confused with a tantrum).

Neurodiversity: Movement that sustains the idea that humans are neurologically diverse due to variations in the human genome.

Neuroplasticity: The brain's ability to form new connections.

Non-verbal: A person who communicates without spoken language. Also refers to communication that is not speech (i.e., body language, touch, pitch, tone, and eye contact)

Occupational Therapy (OT): Therapy to assess and assist people in carrying out everyday activities that are essential to health and well-being, which they may otherwise find difficult. In the case of ASD, OT may focus on fine motor and daily living skills to help create independence for that individual.

PECS (Picture Exchange Communication System): Communication systems use pictures to aid non-verbal individuals.

Physical Therapy: Therapy that focuses on building motor skills and improving balance, strength, and posture.

Proprioception: The brain's capacity to be aware of the location and movement of its individual parts.

Respite Care: Short-term relief for primary caregivers in order to give them free time to rest, travel, or engage in other activities.

Savant Syndrome: Exceptional aptitude in a particular field exhibited by a person who presents an intellectual impairment.

Scripting: Repeating phrases or sentences from movies or books.

Sensory Activity: Activities that stimulate the senses and provide sensory input.

Sensory Diet: Personalized activities to help regulate sensory processing.

Sensory Integration Therapy: Therapy that focuses on improving the sensory processing and integration of the individual through structured sensory experiences and activities.

Sensory Processing Disorder (SPD): A condition in which the brain has difficulty processing and responding to sensory stimuli, leading to changes in daily functioning.

Sensory Room: Space intentionally created to provide sensory resources and stimuli.

(Autistic) Shutdown: Coping mechanism where the autistic person withdraws from their environment. It can be caused by emotional or sensory overwhelm.

Social Story: A narrative is used to prepare and explain social situations.

Self-Advocacy: Ability of an individual to express their own needs, preferences, and goals and to stand up for themselves in different situations.

Speech and Language Therapy (SLT): Therapy that focuses on the treatment and care for individuals with difficulties relating to speech, language, and communication.

Splinter Skill: Specific ability that is disconnected from the context and can't be generalized to other tasks.

Stimming: Self-stimulatory behavior, usually a repetition of sounds or movements, done to obtain sensory input.

Tantrum: Behavior-driven emotional outburst (not to be confused with a meltdown).

Transition Strategies: Techniques to help children smoothly move between activities or environments.

Theory of Mind: The ability to understand that others have beliefs, desires, and intentions that are different from one's own.

Quiet Hands: Encouragement to keep hands still and calm in certain situations.

Visual Supports: Written words, pictures, or icons that convey information in visual medium. Individuals with ASD are typically visual learners and conveying information visually assists with comprehension.

REFERENCES

ABA Centers of Florida. (2022, October 24). *Sensory rooms for autism: 7 amazing benefits!* Abacentersfl.com. https://abacentersfl.com/blog/sensory-rooms-for-autism/

Action For Children. (n.d.). *How can I deal with an autistic meltdown? Action for children.* https://parents.actionforchildren.org.uk/development-additional-needs/neurodiversity/autistic-meltdowns/

Afrin, T. (2022). Resilience in daily routines for children with autism. Resilience in Daily Routines for Children with Autism by Tahera Afrin is licensed under a Creative Commons Attribution-NonCommercial 4.0 International License. *Proceedings: 2021 ITP Research Symposium, 25 and 26 November (Pp. 183–192.* https://doi.org/10.34074/proc.2205014

Allarakha, S. (n.d.). *How does having an autistic child affect the parents?* Medicinenet. https://www.medicinenet.com/how_having_an_autistic_child_affects_the_parents/article.htm

American Academy of Pediatrics. (2016). *What are the early signs of autism?* Healthy Children. https://www.healthychildren.org/English/health-issues/conditions/Autism/Pages/Early-Signs-of-Autism-Spectrum-Disorders.aspx

American Psychological Association. (2021). *Diagnosing and managing autism spectrum disorder (ASD).* APA. https://www.apa.org/topics/autism-spectrum-disorder/diagnosing

American School for the Deaf. (2019, June 26). *The benefits of sensory rooms for children with autism and social/emotional challenges.* American School for the Deaf. https://www.asd-1817.org/news-story?pk=1102483

Anand, N. (2021, February 20). *Common challenges of parenting an autistic child.* Codleo. https://caliberautism.com/blog/Common-Challenges-of-Parenting-an-Autistic-Child

Askham, A. (2020, October 15). *Brain structure changes in autism, explained.* Spectrum. https://www.spectrumnews.org/news/brain-structure-changes-in-autism-explained/

Autism & ADHD Connection. (2021, February 14). *6 ways to boost self-advocacy in your child with autism and ADHD.* Autism & ADHD Connection. https://autismadhdconnection.com/6-ways-to-boost-self-advocacy-in-your-child-with-autism-and-adhd/#google_vignette

Autism Awareness Centre Inc. (2018, September 17). *Advocating for your child at school: Patience and persistence is key.* Autism Awareness. https://autismawarenesscentre.com/advocating-child-school/

Autism Learning Partners. (2020, October 27). *How to set daily routine expectations for your child with autism.* Autism Learning Partners. https://www.autismlearningpartners.com/how-to-set-daily-routine-expectations-for-your-child-with-autism-creating-a-daily-routine-calendar/

Autism Learning Partners. (2022, September 24). *Learning social skills for children with autism.* Autism Learning Partners. https://www.autismlearningpartners.com/learning-social-skills-for-children-with-autism/

Autism Research Institute. (2022, June 28). *Meltdowns & calming techniques in autism.* Autism Research Institute. https://autism.org/meltdowns-calming-techniques-in-autism/

Autism Society of North Carolina. (n.d.). *Autism support groups - Autism support services.* Autism Society of NC. https://www.autismsociety-nc.org/find-chaptersupport-group/

Autism Speaks. (2010). *Your child's rights: Autism and school.* Autism Speaks. https://www.autismspeaks.org/autism-school-your-childs-rights

Autism Speaks. (2018). *Teaching your child self-advocacy.* Autism Speaks. https://www.autismspeaks.org/tool-kit-excerpt/teaching-your-child-self-advocacy

Autism Speaks. (2019). *What are the symptoms of autism?* Autism Speaks. https://www.autismspeaks.org/what-are-symptoms-autism

Autism Specialty Group. (2021, December 24). *Importance of consistency in autism, routine and autism.* Autism Specialty Group. https://www.autismspecialtygroup.com/blog/importance-of-consistency-in-autism

Autism Specialty Group. (2022, April 15). *Autism and change in routine, autism and change of environment.* Autism Specialty Group. https://www.autismspecialtygroup.com/blog/autism-and-change-in-routine

Autism Tasmania. (n.d.). *Social communication.* Autism Tasmania. https://www.autismtas.org.au/about-autism/key-areas-of-difference/social-communication-differences/

Autistic Self Advocacy Network. (2020, June 25). *Your rights in school: A good education for all.* Autistic advocacy. https://autisticadvocacy.org/actioncenter/issues/school/

Ayeni-Bepo, A. (n.d.-a). *5 benefits of advocating for your autistic child at school.* Overcomers Counseling. https://overcomewithus.com/autism/5-benefits-of-advocating-for-your-autistic-child-at-school

Ayeni-Bepo, A. (n.d.-b). *5 grueling challenges of an autistic child's parent.* Overcomers Counseling. https://overcomewithus.com/autism/5-grueling-challenges-of-an-autistic-child-s-parent

Ayeni-Bepo, A. (n.d.-c). *How to plan for your autistic child in case you die.*

Overcomers Counseling. https://overcomewithus.com/autism/how-to-plan-for-your-autistic-child-in-case-you-die

Aylward, L. (2017, March 15). *What are autistic shutdowns and why do they happen?* Bristol Autism Support. https://www.bristolautismsupport.org/autism-autistic-shutdowns/

Babalola, T., Sanguedolce, G., Dipper, L., & Botting, N. (2024). Barriers and facilitators of healthcare access for autistic children in the UK: A systematic review. *Review Journal of Autism and Developmental Disorders.* https://doi.org/10.1007/s40489-023-00420-3

Behavior TLC. (2021, January 5). *5 ways to help your child with autism show empathy.* Behavior TLC. https://behaviortlc.com/blog/help-your-child-with-autism-show-empathy/

Bennie, M. (2016, February 2). *Tantrum vs autistic meltdown: What is the difference?.* Autism Awareness. https://autismawarenesscentre.com/what-is-the-difference-between-a-tantrum-and-an-autistic-meltdown/

Bhandari, S. (2016, December 30). *How do doctors diagnose autism?*; WebMD. https://www.webmd.com/brain/autism/how-do-doctors-diagnose-autism

Biggs, J. (2023, June 1). *Sia opens up about being on the autism spectrum for the first time.* Cosmopolitan. https://www.cosmopolitan.com/uk/body/health/g44048763/celebrities-with-autism/

Brown, J. (2023, September 14). *Emotional regulation: 25 ways to help your autistic child.* Autism Parenting Magazine. https://www.autismparentingmagazine.com/help-child-with-emotional-regulation/

Burner, K. (2013, February 8). *Autism and dealing with change.* The Autism Blog. https://theautismblog.seattlechildrens.org/autism-and-dealing-with-change/

CDC. (2022, March 28). *Signs and symptoms of autism spectrum disorders.* Centers for Disease Control and Prevention. https://www.cdc.gov/ncbddd/autism/signs.html

Centers for Disease Control and Prevention. (2015). *Screening and diagnosis of autism spectrum disorder.* Centers for Disease Control and Prevention. https://www.cdc.gov/ncbddd/autism/screening.html

Centers for Disease Control and Prevention. (2020, March 16). *Accessing services for autism spectrum disorder.* CDC. https://www.cdc.gov/ncbddd/autism/accessing-services-for-autism-spectrum-disorder.html

Collier, E. (2019, January 17). *What is neurodiversity?* The Hub. https://www.highspeedtraining.co.uk/hub/neurodiversity-autism/

cookieslikesmilks. (2023, September 12).Level 1 autistic child - meltdowns at school drop off. Advice? Reddit. https://www.reddit.com/r/Parenting/comments/16gvug5/level_1_autistic_child_meltdowns_at_school_drop/

Courchesne, V., Langlois, V., Gregoire, P., St-Denis, A., Bouvet, L.,

Ostrolenk, A., & Mottron, L. (2020). Interests and strengths in autism, useful but misunderstood: A pragmatic case-study. *Frontiers in Psychology*, *11*. https://doi.org/10.3389/fpsyg.2020.569339

Currigan, S. (2020, October 12). *How to teach empathy to kids with autism*. Beacon School Support. https://beaconschoolsupport.co.uk/newsletters/how-to-teach-empathy-to-kids-with-autism

Davis-Pierre, M. (2022, April 7). *Helping children with autism connect with emotions*. PBS KIDS for Parents. https://www.pbs.org/parents/thrive/helping-children-with-autism-connect-with-emotions

Delano, C. (2021, July 29). *Autism shutdown: The causes and how to manage it*. Autism Parenting Magazine. https://www.autismparentingmagazine.com/manage-autism-shutdown/

Denworth, L. (2019, June 26). *Social communication in autism, explained*. Spectrum. https://www.spectrumnews.org/news/social-communication-autism-explained/

Deron School. (2015, June 25). *How to choose the right education for your autistic child*. Deron School. https://www.deronschool.org/tips/how-to-choose-the-right-education-for-your-autistic-child/

Deweerdt, S. (2020, January 31). *Repetitive behaviors and "stimming" in autism, explained*. Spectrum. https://www.spectrumnews.org/news/repetitive-behaviors-and-stimming-in-autism-explained/

Dream Big Children's Center. (2021, February 10). *The incredible benefits of early intervention for children with autism*. Dream Big Children's Center. https://dreambigchildren.com/the-incredible-benefits-of-early-intervention-for-children-with-autism/

Easterseals. (n.d.). *Glossary of autism spectrum disorders related terminology*. Easter Seals. https://www.easterseals.com/support-and-education/living-with-autism/glossary-of-autism-disorders.html

Elemy. (2020a, May 19). *Autism statistics & rates in 2022*. Elemy. https://elemy.wpengine.com/autism/statistics-and-rates

Elemy. (2020b, May 30). *5 ways to improve social skills for autistic children*. Elemy. https://elemy.wpengine.com/autism-family-guide/improve-social-skills

Elkin, R. (2022, November 8). *Higher or lower? Why using functional labels to describe autism is problematic*. Psychiatry-UK. https://psychiatry-uk.com/higher-or-lower-why-using-functional-labels-to-describe-autism-is-problematic/

Erie County Care Management. (n.d.). *Difference between developmental delays and autism*. ECCM. https://www.eccm.org/blog/difference-between-developmental-delays-and-autism

Experia USA. (2020, October 12). *Five ways an ASD sensory room can help children*. Experia USA. https://www.experia-usa.com/blog/five-ways-an-asd-sensory-room-can-help-children/

Ferguson, S. (2022, December 15). *Common autism misdiagnoses: Signs, risk factors, and consequences*. Healthline. https://www.healthline.com/health/autism/autism-misdiagnosis

Friedman, S., & Morrison, S. A. (2021). *"I just want to stay out there all day": A case study of two special educators and five autistic children learning outside at school*. Frontiers in Education, 6. https://doi.org/10.3389/feduc.2021.668991

Friend In Me. (n.d.). *Friend in me*. Friendinmegroup. https://www.friendin megroup.org/

Ganassini, V. (2014, March 31). *How do I teach a person with asd to be more independent?* Autism Awareness. https://autismawarenesscentre.com/teach-person-asd-independent/

Gans, S. (2023, November 29). *Does my autistic adult child need a guardian?* Verywell health. https://www.verywellhealth.com/legal-rights-of-autis tic-adults-4165687

Gehret, M. (2019, November 6). *Issues with defining "high" and "low" functioning autism*. SPE. https://spectrumofhope.com/defining-high-and-low-functioning-autism/

Gehret, M. (2022, August 10). *Tips for creating routines for a child with autism*. Spectrum of Hope Houston. https://spectrumofhope.com/blog/create-routine-for-kids-with-autism/

Goally. (2023a, May 30). *How to create an autism daily routine*. Goally Apps for Kids. https://getgoally.com/blog/how-to-create-an-autism-daily-routine/

Goally. (2023b, December 12). *Do's and don't's of dealing with autistic melt-downs*. Goally apps & tablets for kids. https://getgoally.com/blog/autistic-meltdowns/

Golden User. (2022, March 30). *Autism and empathy in children*. Golden Care. https://www.goldencaretherapy.com/autism-and-empathy-in-chil dren/

Gordon, D. (2009, September). *Seeing the benefits of early intervention in autism*. Brainandlife. https://www.brainandlife.org/articles/early-inter vention-in-autism

Grand Valley State University. (n.d.). *Family and school collaboration- Autism - START project*. Grand Valley State University. https://www.gvsu.edu/autismcenter/collaborating-with-your-school-team-247.htm

Green, J. (2023). Debate: Neurodiversity, autism and healthcare. *Child and Adolescent Mental Health, 28*(3), 438–442. https://doi.org/10.1111/camh.12663

Gunter, P. L., Fox, J. J., McEvoy, M. A., Shores, R. E., & Denny, R. K. (1993).A case study of the reduction of aberrant, repetitive responses of an adolescent with autism. *Education and Treatment of Children, 16*(2), 187–197. https://www.jstor.org/stable/42899308

Ha, S., Sohn, I.-J., Kim, N., Sim, H. J., & Cheon, K.-A. (2015). Characteristics of brains in autism spectrum disorder: Structure, function and connectivity across the lifespan. *Experimental Neurobiology, 24*(4), 273. https://doi.org/10.5607/en.2015.24.4.273

Hands Center for Autism. (2022, June 28). *Common challenges parents of children with autism face.* Handscenter. https://www.handscenter.com/common-challenges-parents-of-children-with-autism-face

Harsha Autism Center. (2023, September 10). *Working together: How parents can collaborate with school teachers for the benefit of their autistic child.* Harsha Autism Center. https://harshaautism.com/working-together-how-parents-can-collaborate-with-school-teachers-for-the-benefit-of-their-autistic-child/

Hazelton, M. (2021, March 9). *What if I'm failing my son with autism?* Her view from home. https://herviewfromhome.com/what-if-im-failing-my-son/

Heidel, J. A. (2021, August 19). *Navigating autistic meltdowns - a dos and don'ts guide.* The Articulate Autistic. https://www.thearticulateautistic.com/navigating-autistic-meltdowns-a-dos-and-donts-guide/

Hopebridge. (2019, September 24). *10 easy sensory activities for children with autism.* Hopebridge Autism Therapy Center. https://www.hopebridge.com/blog/10-easy-sensory-activities/

Hopper, D. (2019, March 31). *How to create a sensory-safe home for your autistic child.* Life skills 4 kids. https://www.lifeskills4kids.com.au/create-sensory-safe-home-autistic-child/

Hosseinpour, A., Younesi, S. J., Azkhosh, M., Safi, M. H., & Biglarian, A. (2022). Exploring challenges and needs of parents providing care to children with autism spectrum disorders: A qualitative study. *Iranian Journal of Psychiatry and Behavioral Sciences, 16*(3). https://doi.org/10.5812/ijpbs-127300

Hutten, M. (n.d.). *Feeling like a "bad" parent of a child on the autism spectrum.* My ASD Child. https://www.myaspergerschild.com/2017/11/feeling-like-bad-parent-of-child-on.html

IAHP. (2022, March 10). *Autism: A story of hope.* IAHP. https://iahp.org/autism-story-hope-alex-goes-way/

IfeelloveIfeellove. (2018, October 3). *High vs low on the spectrum is bullshit.* Reddit. https://www.reddit.com/r/autism/comments/9kznum/high_vs_low_on_the_spectrum_is_bullshit/

Keltner, D. (2023, April 3). *Temple Grandin shares her journey with autism.* Greater Good. https://greatergood.berkeley.edu/article/item/temple_grandin_shares_her_journey_with_autism

Kenny, K. (2023a, July 19). *How to advocate for your child with autism spectrum disorder (ASD) in.* Dr. Noze Best. https://drnozebest.com/blogs/the-doctor-is-in/how-to-advocate-for-your-child-with-autism-spectrum-disorder-asd-in-a-medical-setting

Kenny, K. (2023b, December 18). *Healthcare barriers of those with asd (And how to overcome them).* Dr. Noze Best. https://drnozebest.com/blogs/the-doctor-is-in/healthcare-barriers-of-those-with-autism-spectrum-disorder-and-strategies-to-manage-them

Kim, S. H., & Lord, C. (2010). Restricted and repetitive behaviors in toddlers and preschoolers with autism spectrum disorders based on the Autism Diagnostic Observation Schedule (ADOS). *Autism Research,* 3(4), 162–173. https://doi.org/10.1002/aur.142

Kozlowski, C. (2017, July 5). *How to create a sensory room for kids with autism.* Autism Parenting Magazine. https://www.autismparentingmagazine.com/creating-sensory-space-for-asd-kids/

LaGasse, B. (2017). Social outcomes in children with autism spectrum disorder: a review of music therapy outcomes. *Patient Related Outcome Measures, Volume 8*(8), 23–32. https://doi.org/10.2147/prom.s106267

Lewis, L. F., & Stevens, K. (2023). The lived experience of meltdowns for autistic adults. *Autism,* 27(6), 136236132211457. https://doi.org/10.1177/13623613221145783

Lisa Jo Rudy. (2010, April). *What makes an autistic person a savant?* Verywell health. https://www.verywellhealth.com/what-is-an-autistic-savant-260033

Lisa Jo Rudy. (2019). *Is there really such a thing as high and low functioning autism?* Verywell Health. https://www.verywellhealth.com/high-and-low-functioning-autism-260599

Lively, I. (2023, March 31). *What are autistic shutdowns? (Adults and kids).* A day in our shoes. https://adayinourshoes.com/autistic-shutdown/

Lober, G. (2015). *Scholarworks at WMU autism spectrum disorder: A case study of Mikey.* https://scholarworks.wmich.edu/cgi/viewcontent.cgi?article=3638&context=honors_theses

Loftus, Y. (2022, June 3). *Autism guardianship and alternative options to consider.* Autism Parenting Magazine. https://www.autismparentingmagazine.com/autism-guardianship-alternative/

Loos Miller, I. M., & Loos, H. G. (2015, October 15). *Shutdowns and stress in autism.* Autism Awareness. https://autismawarenesscentre.com/shutdowns-stress-autism/

Louise , M. (1970, January 1). *"it's all my fault!" Understanding guilt in parents of children with ASD.* Autism Spectrum News. https://autismspec trumnews.org/its-all-my-fault-understanding-guilt-in-parents-of-chil dren-with-asd/

LuxAi. (2021, March 17). *How to teach emotion recognition and labelling to children with autism.* LuxAI S.A. https://luxai.com/blog/emotion-recognition-for-autism/

Maddox, B. B., Dickson, K. S., Stadnick, N. A., Mandell, D. S., & Brookman-Frazee, L. (2021). Mental health services for autistic individuals across the lifespan: Recent advances and current gaps. *Current Psychiatry Reports, 23*(10). https://doi.org/10.1007/s11920-021-01278-0

Making Autistic Friendships. (n.d.). *MAF.* Makingauthenticfriendships. https://www.makingauthenticfriendships.com/

Malc, L. (2020, December 7). *Red flags for autism: 8 behaviours to look for.* Side by side ABA therapy near me. https://www.sidebysidetherapy.ca/autism-spectrum-disorder/red-flags-for-autism-8-behaviours-to-look-for/

Malcolm, R. (2022, May 10).Choosing the best educational option for your autistic child. Autism Parenting Magazine. https://www.autismparent ingmagazine.com/best-educational-option/

Malik-Soni, N., Shaker, A., Luck, H., Mullin, A. E., Wiley, R. E., Lewis, M. E. S., Fuentes, J., & Frazier, T. W. (2021). Tackling healthcare access barriers for individuals with autism from diagnosis to adulthood. *Pediatric Research, 91*(5), 1028–1035. https://doi.org/10.1038/s41390-021-01465-y

Marcus Autism Center. (n.d.). *Establishing routines at home.* Marcus Autism Center. https://www.marcus.org/autism-resources/autism-tips-and-resources/establishing-routines-at-home

marketing.admin. (2021, July 7). *Tantrum vs autistic meltdown: What is the difference? How to deal with them?* LuxAI S.A. https://luxai.com/blog/tantrum-vs-autistic-meltdown/

Merriam-Webster. (2019). *Definition of advocacy.* Merriam-Webster.com. Retrieved March 11, 2024, from https://www.merriam-webster.com/dictionary/advocacy

michelfmc30. (2022, June 18). *How frustrated do you guys get with changes in routines?* Reddit. https://www.reddit.com/r/AutismTranslated/comments/vewb3w/how_frustrated_do_you_guys_get_with_changes_in/

Middletown Centre for Autism. (n.d.-a). *Case study 1.* Best Practice: Sensory. https://sensory-processing.middletownautism.com/casestudies/case-study-1/

Middletown Centre for Autism. (n.d.-b). *Case study 5.* Best Practice:

Sensory. https://sensory-processing.middletownautism.com/casestudies/case-study-5/

Milam, S. (2018, April 18). *When my son with autism melts down, here's what I do.* Healthline Media. https://www.healthline.com/health/autism/what-to-do-autism-meltdown

Morris-Clarke, C. (2020, June 17). *Social communication and children on the autism spectrum.* Living Autism. https://livingautism.com/social-communication-autism/

Mulligan, E. (n.d.). *PFA tips: 10 ways to build independence.* Pathfinders for Autism. https://pathfindersforautism.org/articles/advocacy/pfa-tips-10-ways-to-build-independence/

My Autism Team. (2013, June 13). *Should I get a second opinion?* My Autism Team. https://www.myautismteam.com/questions/51ba2c021fcaa31aa10017dc/should-i-get-a-second-opinion

My World ABA. (2023, September 15). *Empowering autistic children: Tips for building independence.* My World ABA. https://myworldaba.com/2023/09/15/empowering-autistic-children-tips-for-building-their-independence/

National Autistic Society. (2020, August 14). *Obsessions and repetitive behaviour - a guide for all audiences.* Autism.org. https://www.autism.org.uk/advice-and-guidance/topics/behaviour/obsessions/all-audiences

National Autistic Society. (2023). *Autistic women and girls.* Autism.org. https://www.autism.org.uk/advice-and-guidance/what-is-autism/autistic-women-and-girls

National Institutes of Health. (2017, January 31). *Early intervention for autism.* NICHD. https://www.nichd.nih.gov/health/topics/autism/conditioninfo/treatments/early-intervention

nearlyhalfabicycle. (2018, January 30). *For the people here who ask if you can be autistic and be able to read emotions.* Reddit. https://www.reddit.com/r/aspergers/comments/7u0n0i/for_the_people_here_who_ask_if_you_can_be/

Neustadt, R. (2022, December 21). *How to manage stress as a parent of a child with autism.* Circle Care Services. https://circlecareservices.com/how-to-manage-stress-as-a-parent-of-a-child-with-autism/

NHS. (2022, November 11). *Signs of autism in children.* NHS. https://www.nhs.uk/conditions/autism/signs/children/

O'Lone, K. (2023, August 16). *Creating a sensory-friendly home for autistic children.* WonderBaby. https://www.wonderbaby.org/articles/sensory-friendly-home

Online Master of Science in Behavioral Psychology program from Pepperdine University. (2018, December 3). *How to improve emotional self-regulation among children with autism and attention disorders.* Onlinegrad.pepperdine.edu. https://onlinegrad.pepperdine.edu/blog/emotional-self-regulation-children-autism/

Organization for Autism Research. (2016, June 1). *Help children learn how to self advocate*. Organization for Autism Research. https://researchautism.org/blog/help-children-learn-how-to-self-advocate/

Orlowsky & Wilson. (2022, December 19). *Why a special needs trust is crucial for autistic children*. Orlowsky & Wilson. https://orlowskywilson.com/why-a-special-needs-trust-is-crucial-for-autistic-children/

Orpwood, M. (2017, July). *Five challenges for parents of autistic children*. WeHaveKids. https://wehavekids.com/parenting/The-Many-Faces-of-a-Special-Needs-Parent

Otsimo. (2017, May 30). *Legal education rights of children with autism in the USA*. Otsimo. https://otsimo.com/en/autism-legal/

Otsimo Editorial Team. (2019, March 17). *Autism empathy and social cues*. Otsimo. https://otsimo.com/en/autism-empathy-social-cues/

pak4z0r0. (2023, September 19). *Parents, how did you teach your children to handle emotions?* Reddit. https://www.reddit.com/r/aspergers/comments/16myjdx/parents_how_did_you_teach_your_children_to_handle/

Papahuma. (2022, February 27). *How does it feel to have autism?* Reddit. https://www.reddit.com/r/autism/comments/t2qqnx/how_does_it_feel_to_have_autism/

Patel, S. (2019). *Autistic meltdowns and how to avoid them*. Verywell Health. https://www.verywellhealth.com/what-is-an-autistic-meltdown-260154

Pedersen, T. (2022, April 29). *Autism misdiagnosis: What is autism often misdiagnosed as?* Psych Central. https://psychcentral.com/autism/autism-misdiagnosis

Performance Health. (n.d.). *How to create a sensory room on a budget*. Performance Health. https://www.performancehealth.com/articles/how-to-create-a-sensory-room-on-a-budget

Psychology Today. (n.d.). *Neurodiversity and the benefits of autism*. Psychology Today South Africa. Retrieved February 26, 2024, from https://www.psychologytoday.com/za/basics/autism/neurodiversity-and-the-benefits-autism

Quora. (2019). *Should we be teaching kids with autism social skills or should we just let them be?* Quora. https://www.quora.com/Should-we-be-teaching-kids-with-autism-social-skills-or-should-we-just-let-them-be

Raising Children Network. (2017a, January 31). *Family stress and autism spectrum disorder*. Raising Children Network. https://raisingchildren.net.au/autism/communicating-relationships/family-relationships/family-stress-asd

Raising Children Network. (2017b, August 2). *Social skills for children with*

autism spectrum disorder. Raising Children Network. https://raisingchil
dren.net.au/autism/communicating-relationships/connecting/social-
skills-for-children-with-asd

Raising Children Network. (2020). *Changing routines: children and teenagers
with autism spectrum disorder*. Raising Children Network. https://rais
ingchildren.net.au/autism/behaviour/understanding-behaviour/chang
ing-routines-asd

Raising Children Network. (2022a, April 28). *Meltdowns: autistic children and
teenagers*. Raising Children Network. https://raisingchildren.net.au/
autism/behaviour/common-concerns/meltdowns-autistic-children-
teenagers

Raising Children Network. (2022b, April 28). *Recognising, understanding and
managing emotions: Autistic children and teenagers*. Raising Children
Network.   https://raisingchildren.net.au/autism/development/social-
emotional-development/recognising-understanding-emotions-autistic-
children-teens

Rizzo, N. (2019, August 13). *5 tips for choosing the right school for your child
with autism*. RCS consulting. https://rcsconsultingne.com/5-tips-for-
choosing-the-right-school-for-your-child-with-autism/

Rossi, C. (2021, May 7). *Autism spectrum disorder: Autistic brains vs non-autistic
brains*. Psycom.net. https://www.psycom.net/autism-brain-differences

Rothman, B. (2013, February 22). *Autism is not a parenting fail*. HuffPost.
https://www.huffpost.com/entry/autism_b_2733094

Rudy, L. J. (2010, June). *Repetitive behaviors in autism*. Verywell Health.
https://www.verywellhealth.com/repetitive-behaviors-in-autism-260582

Rudy, L. J. (2017, February 23). *Autistic children and developmental milestones*.
Verywell Health. https://www.verywellhealth.com/developmental-mile
stones-in-children-with-autism-4128725

Rudy, L. J. (2019). *How autism may affect sympathy and empathy*. Verywell
Health.   https://www.verywellhealth.com/do-people-with-autism-lack-
empathy-259887

Rudy, L. J. (2022, February 23). *Even kids with very high functioning autism
have emotional meltdowns*. Verywell Health. https://www.verywellhealth.
com/helping-children-with-autism-handle-emotions-260146

Sarris, M. (2014, April 8). *Coming of age: Autism and the transition to adulthood*.
Kennedykrieger.   https://www.kennedykrieger.org/stories/interactive-
autism-network-ian/autism-transition-to-adulthood

Sarris, M. (2015, November 12). *Coming of age: Autism and the transition to
adulthood*. SPARK for Autism. https://sparkforautism.org/discover_arti
cle/coming-of-age-autism-and-the-transition-to-adulthood/

Saxena, S. (2021). *Removing provider and system level barriers to better support autistic people*. UPENN. https://hosting.med.upenn.edu/cmh/removing-barriers-for-autistic-people/

Shore, A. (2018, March 31). *How people with autism see the world*. News at Curtin. https://www.curtin.edu.au/news/people-autism-see-world/

Silveira-Zaldivara, T., Özerk, G., & Özerk, K. (2021). Developing social skills and social competence in children with autism. *International Electronic Journal of Elementary Education, 13*(3), 341–363. https://doi.org/10.26822/iejee.2021.195

Smith, K. (2020, February 5). *Coping with stress while caring for a child with autism*. Psycom.net. https://www.psycom.net/coping-with-stress-while-caring-for-a-child-with-autism

Special Learning. (2021, November 22). *IMportance of love and patience*. Special Learning. https://special-learning.com/importance-of-love-and-patience/

St. Clair, A. (n.d.). *Special needs trusts*. Autism Speaks. https://www.autismspeaks.org/tool-kit-excerpt/special-needs-trusts

Steinberg Behavior Solutions. (2021, March 3). *Five tips for being an effective advocate for your child with autism in the school setting - Steinberg behavior solutions*. Https://Www.sbsaba.com/. https://www.sbsaba.com/five-tips-for-being-an-effective-advocate-for-your-child-with-autism-in-the-school-setting/

strawberrymilfshake7. (2023, September 21). *Sensory room*. Reddit. https://www.reddit.com/r/Autism_Parenting/comments/16of7kw/sensory_room/

Syriopoulou-Delli, C. K., Cassimos, D. C., & Polychronopoulou, S. A. (2016). Collaboration between teachers and parents of children with ASD on issues of education. *Research in Developmental Disabilities, 55*(August 2016), 330–345. https://doi.org/10.1016/j.ridd.2016.04.011

Ten ways to create a sensory-friendly environment for children. (2023, September 27). Family Matters. https://familymatters-uk.co.uk/ten-ways-to-create-a-sensory-friendly-environment-for-children/

The Autism Page. (2017, May 19). *Glossary*. The Autism Page. https://www.theautismpage.com/contact/

The Autism Project. (n.d.). *Social groups*. The Autism Project. https://theautismproject.org/parents-families/programs-resources/social-groups

The Autism Site. (2017, October 21). *8 tips for developing patience with your child*. The Autism Site News. https://blog.theautismsite.greatergood.com/cs-patience-with-child/

The Editors of Encyclopaedia Britannica. (2019). *Temple Grandin | American scientist and industrial designer*. Encyclopædia Britannica. https://www.britannica.com/biography/Temple-Grandin

The FCA. (2022). *10 fun sensory activities for a child with autism*. The FCA. https://www.thefca.co.uk/fostering-autistic-children/sensory-activities-children-autism/

The Lovaas Center. (n.d.). *Being an effective advocate for your child with autism*. The Lovaas Center. https://thelovaascenter.com/aba-treatment/advo cacy-for-a-child-with-autism/

The Place for Children with Autism. (n.d.). *Developmental milestone delay – Signs of autism in children*. The place for children with autism. https://thep laceforchildrenwithautism.com/what-is-autism/signs-of-autism-in-chil dren/autism-developmental-delay

The Star Academy. (2024, February 7). *Choosing an education program for your child on the spectrum*. The Star Academy. https://thestaracademy.co. za/choosing-an-education-program/

The Treffert Center. (2021). *Savant syndrome*. SSMHealth. https://www. ssmhealth.com/treffert-center/conditions-treatments/savant-syndrome

Therapeutic Pathways. (2021, May 7). *Why children with autism need routines at home*. Therapeutic Pathways. https://www.tpathways.org/blog/why-children-with-autism-need-routines/

Toth, K. E. (2011, August 10). *Social skills and autism*. The Autism Blog. https://theautismblog.seattlechildrens.org/social-skills-and-autism/

ToughCookie00. (2023, June 18). *I was screwed over big time by a false autism diagnosis, and I'm furious*. Reddit. https://www.reddit.com/r/ADHD/ comments/14cg20g/i_was_screwed_over_big_time_by_a_false_autism/

Treffert, D. A. (2009). The savant syndrome: an extraordinary condition. A synopsis: past, present, future. *Philosophical Transactions of the Royal Society B: Biological Sciences, 364*(1522), 1351–1357. https://doi.org/10. 1098/rstb.2008.0326

Vicker, B. (n.d.). *Social communication and language characteristics associated with high functioning, verbal children and adults with ASD: Articles: Indiana Resource Center for Autism: Indiana University Bloomington*. Indiana Resource Center for Autism. https://www.iidc.indiana.edu/irca/articles/ social-communication-and-language-characteristics.html

violetstarlights. (2023, February 22). *Autistic shutdowns- how long do they last?* Reddit. https://www.reddit.com/r/neurodiversity/comments/118oj2n/ autistic_shutdowns_how_long_do_they_last/

Wilson, L. (2023a, April 24). *Special needs trusts*. The autism community in action. https://tacanow.org/family-resources/special-needs-trusts/

Wilson, L. (2023b, April 26). *Legal planning and autism*. The autism commu-nity in action. https://tacanow.org/family-resources/legal-planning-and-autism/

Zauderer, S. (2023a, September 18). *14 sensory activities for a child with autism*. Cross River Therapy. https://www.crossrivertherapy.com/autism/sensory-activities

Zauderer, S. (2023b, September 19). *Autism routines: Why children with ASD like routines*. Cross River Therapy. https://www.crossrivertherapy.com/autism/routines

Made in the USA
Las Vegas, NV
27 May 2024

90445509R00098